G.O.A.T.

MAKING THE CASE FOR THE GREATEST OF ALL TIME

LEBRON JAMES

BY BOB GURNETT

STERLING CHILDREN'S BOOKS
New York

STERLING CHILDREN'S BOOKS
New York

An Imprint of Sterling Publishing Co., Inc.
1166 Avenue of the Americas
New York, NY 10036

STERLING'S CHILDREN'S BOOKS and the distinctive Sterling Children' logo are registered trademarks of Sterling Publishing Co., Inc.

Text © 2019 Bob Gurnett

Cover photograph by Adam Pantozzi/©NBAE/Getty Images

All rights reserved. No part of this publication may be reproduced, stored in a retrieval system, or transmitted in any form or by any means (including electronic, mechanical, photocopying, recording, or otherwise) without prior written permission from the publisher.

ISBN 978-1-4549-3098-3

Distributed in Canada by Sterling Publishing Co., Inc.
c/o Canadian Manda Group, 664 Annette Street
Toronto, Ontario M6S 2C8, Canada
Distributed in the United Kingdom by GMC Distribution Services
Castle Place, 166 High Street, Lewes, East Sussex BN7 1XU, England
Distributed in Australia by NewSouth Books
University of New South Wales, Sydney, NSW 2052, Australia

For information about custom editions, special sales, and premium and corporate purchases, please contact Sterling Special Sales at 800-805-5489 or specialsales@sterlingpublishing.com.

Manufactured in China

Lot #:
4 6 8 10 9 7 5
04/21

sterlingpublishing.com

Cover and interior design by Heather Kelly

Image credits are on page 128

CONTENTS

	WHAT IS A G.O.A.T?	5
1	A BOY NAMED BRON BRON	7
2	HIGH SCHOOL SUPERSTAR	13
3	WITNESS A GREAT START	29
4	POSTSEASON LEBRON	43
5	MOST VALUABLE LEBRON	55
6	TAKING HIS TALENTS TO SOUTH BEACH	63
7	LEBRON'S BIG THREE	67
8	RETURN OF THE KING	80
9	AWARDS AND RECOGNITION	89
10	RECORDS AND STATS	92
11	RIVALRIES	97
12	WHO ELSE?	107
13	WHAT THE FUTURE HOLDS	114
	GLOSSARY	117
	BIBLIOGRAPHY	120
	INDEX	126
	IMAGE CREDITS	128

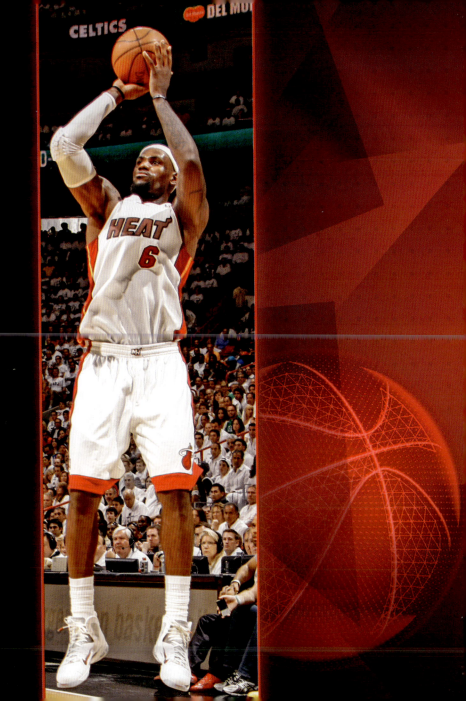

WHAT IS A
G.O.A.T?

Most people do not want to be compared to a barnyard animal, but a G.O.A.T is different. These G.O.A.T.s aren't found in petting zoos, but you can see them on the gridiron, the hardwood, the ice, and the diamond. G.O.A.T. is an acronym that stands for **G**reatest **O**f **A**ll **T**ime. It takes lifelong dedication, non-stop hard work, and undeniable talent just to become a professional athlete. But to become the greatest of all time, well, that's nearly impossible. There are a handful of athletes who are widely thought to be the G.O.A.T of their sport. Swimmer Michael Phelps moves like a fish in water, but he is also the G.O.A.T. with 23 Olympic gold medals, the most of all time. Tennis player Serena Williams is the G.O.A.T. with 23 Grand Slam titles in the Open Era, more than any woman *or* man.

But for some sports, a G.O.A.T is not as easy to identify and fans may disagree. If you asked five baseball lovers who the greatest baseball player of all time is,

G.O.A.T. LEBRON JAMES

you might get five different answers. Babe Ruth, Willie Mays, Barry Bonds, Cy Young, Lou Gehrig, or when it's all said and done, maybe rising young superstar Mike Trout. The G.O.A.T can change depending on who is asked, and what their reasons, or criteria, are. Babe Ruth won seven World Series, had a .342 batting average for his career, and is still in 3rd place all time for home runs, even though he retired over 80 years ago in 1935. Willie Mays did not have the same bat as Ruth, but he is still considered the best defensive player in history. Different players, different achievements, but both still considered the greatest at what they did. Fans will disagree on who the true G.O.A.T. is, but to even be considered, a player must be one of the best to ever live.

Basketball has its own G.O.A.T. debate. Many people think Michael Jordan, the six-time champion who never lost in the NBA Finals, is the best. Some say it's Wilt Chamberlain, the only player to score 100 points in a game. Others still will say it is no doubt the all-time scoring leader, Kareem Abdul-Jabbar, or Bill Russell, who won the most NBA championships ever.. It very well may be that the NBA's G.O.A.T. is playing right now! At the top of his game is NBA superstar, LeBron "the King" James, basketball's Greatest Of All Time? Let's review the evidence to find out!

1

A BOY NAMED BRON BRON

Before LeBron James ever bounced a basketball, he was a bouncing baby boy. On December 30, 1984 in Akron, Ohio, Gloria James gave birth to LeBron Raymone James. There was no way Gloria could have known that her tiny baby would grow up to be the Akron Hammer, the King, or to many, the greatest basketball player of all time.

LeBron's childhood was anything but regal. He came from humble and difficult beginnings. His mother moved them from apartment to apartment in the poorest areas of Akron. By age 8, LeBron and his mother had moved ten times! LeBron spent many nights sleeping on couches as they struggled to find their way. This nomadic lifestyle made it hard for LeBron James to make friends, and there just wasn't enough money for him to play

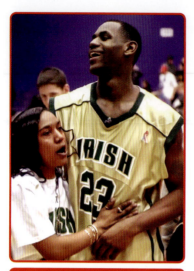

LeBron and his mother when he was in high school

organized sports. The idea that LeBron James, one of the greatest athletes of all time, never played on a sports team until he was eight years old may be mind-blowing, but it is true! Instead, LeBron played sandlot football with neighborhood kids. And when a Pee Wee football coach offered to pay for his equipment and drive him to games, LeBron and his mother jumped at the opportunity.

LeBron was shy and awkward as a kid. Much taller than his peers, he would rather spend his time in the back of the classroom than in the spotlight. That began to change when he started playing organized football at eight years old. On the first play with his new team, the boy who everyone knew as "Bron Bron" ran the ball 80 yards for a touchdown. He played running back for the select East Dragons football team. The quiet kid who had been to eight different schools and spent many nights sleeping on couches was finally finding his place. LeBron's Pee Wee coach, Bruce Kelker, even opened his home to LeBron and his mother. Young Bron Bron's life

A BOY NAMED BRON BRON

started to gain stability. Coach Kelker was happy to offer LeBron and Gloria a home, despite the fact that he thought LeBron had stinky feet. LeBron finished that season with 17 touchdowns, each one scored with his mom running along the sideline, cheering his name. Because he moved so often, LeBron had always been the new kid at school and just wanted to blend in. It was while playing Pee Wee football that LeBron learned that he was destined to stand out.

After football season, another coach, Frankie Walker, invited LeBron and Gloria to live with him. Since football was over, Walker wanted LeBron to try his hand at basketball. Walker matched young LeBron against his son, also named Frankie, in a game of 21. LeBron got crushed. The future NBA champion lost in an embarrassing 21–7 game. He couldn't dribble. He couldn't make a left-handed layup. Though he was tall, without training LeBron was not going to win against Frankie. But Coach Walker took LeBron James under his wing and taught him the fundamentals. Next time you see LeBron finish a layup with his left hand, you can thank Frankie Walker.

By middle school, LeBron and his mom had their own place again, but LeBron would frequently spend the night at the Walkers' home. He had become a part of their family and continued to learn basketball from

Frankie well into middle school. By then, LeBron played for the Shooting Stars, an Amateur Athletic Union (AAU) team, a national private club for outstanding young athletes. They had already won a bunch of national championships. The Shooting Stars were an elite squad, but the highlight of LeBron's middle school career was during a teacher-student charity game. The game was played each year, and the teachers were undefeated. LeBron made them nervous. By 8th grade, he was already six feet tall, taller than some of the teachers he was playing! The teachers may have been historically undefeated, but so was LeBron's AAU team, the Shooting Stars. LeBron and three other teammates had been nicknamed the Fab Four. They proved to be too fast for the teachers, who were winded and wheezing early into the game. The boys quickly took a 20-point lead over the teachers. In the stands, the students were going wild, cheering for what appeared to be an exciting upset in the making. The fans watching had no idea that they were about to witness history. Late in the game, LeBron stole the ball from a teacher in the backcourt. There was nobody between him and the basket. He raced down the court. He rose up from a full sprint. He reached just over the rim and slammed the ball down. It was LeBron's first dunk ever and it sent the crowd into chaos. It was not

A BOY NAMED BRON BRON

the signature, thundering dunks that NBA LeBron fans are used to, but for an 8th grader, it was an incredible feat. After the game, the teachers took down the rim and saved it as a memento. LeBron's coaches, friends, and family knew he was something special, and with that dunk, LeBron advertised to all of Ohio that he was a superstar in the making.

LeBron dunking in high school

2

HIGH SCHOOL SUPERSTAR

LeBron won six AAU national championships in middle school. He was one of the best AAU players in history. He was ready for newer and bigger challenges. Lucky for him, it was time for him to move on to high school. In high school, all the players are bigger, faster, and more experienced. The change is hard for everyone, even LeBron. Luckily, all of the Fab Four decided to go to the same school, St. Vincent–St. Mary's, instead of a nearby high school with a better basketball program. LeBron did not want to break up the Fab Four. He wanted to win with his friends. LeBron's loyalty and desire to play with his friends would follow him all the way to the NBA.

In their first year, all of the Fab Four made the varsity team, but LeBron was the only one to start. He was the first

G.O.A.T. LEBRON JAMES

freshman starter for the St. Vincent–St. Mary Fighting Irish in years. Even Michael Jordan didn't make his varsity team until he was a junior. In basketball, a **starter** plays at the beginning of the game and they usually get more minutes than players who are come in off the bench. Most teams start their very best players. Even though LeBron was a starting guard on the varsity basketball team, he was still a shy, nervous 14-year-old. However, he had sprouted to six foot four and 170 pounds! Only one year out of middle school, and he was already as big as a lot of the seniors!

BASKETBALL STATISTICS

Many sports fans love statistics. They help fans understand who does what on the basketball court. The basic stats you will see most are points scored, rebounds, and assists. Rebounds are when a player grabs a ball after a missed shot. Assists are when a player passes the ball to a teammate in a way that sets them up to score. In the NBA, statisticians sit on the sideline and track these numbers and others. During the game a scorekeeper makes a box score from these stats. That box score shows all statistics from the game. Every rebound, every assist, every point scored. All those numbers are accounted for. Let's break down what goes into a box score and what those statistics mean.

STARTERS	MIN	FGA	FGM	3PT	FTA	FTM	OREB	REB	AST	STL	BLK	TO	PF	+/-	PTS
L. James	43	30	16	4-8	8	5	4	16	7	3	3	2	1	+13	49

HIGH SCHOOL SUPERSTAR

STARTERS/BENCH—The players who started the game will be listed first with the players who came off the bench under them.

MIN—Minutes played.

FGA—Field Goals Attempted. This is how many shots the player took.

FGM—Field Goals Made. How many shots the player made.

3PT—How many 3 pointers the player made.

FTA—Free Throws Attempted.

FTM—Free Throws Made.

OREB—Offensive Rebounds. How many times a player rebounded the ball from their team's missed shot.

DREB—Defensive Rebounds. How many times a player rebounded the ball from the other team's missed shot.

REB—Rebounds.

AST—Assists. How many times a player passes the ball to a teammate in a way that sets them up to score.

STL—Steals. How many times a player takes the ball for the other team usually by taking it from them or intercepting a pass.

BLK—Blocks. How many times a player hits a ball shot by the other team, causing it to miss.

TO—Turnovers. How many times a player loses the ball to the other team, either by bad pass or penalty.

PF—Personal fouls. How many times a player hits or bumps another player in a way that is illegal. In the NBA, a player is ejected on the 6th PF.

+/-—Plus/Minus. This number shows the scoring difference while a player is on the court. Positive numbers mean their team outscored the other team by that many points, a negative means they were outscored.

PTS—Points.

At the bottom of the box score, all columns are added up to show the totals for the team.

15

G.O.A.T. LEBRON JAMES

In LeBron's first high school game on December 3rd, 1999, he scored 15 points and pulled down 8 rebounds in a blowout win over Cuyahoga Falls. For any player, this was a great game, but for a 14-year-old freshman playing his first game on a varsity team, it was unheard of. He was years younger than many of his opponents, yet he used his size, explosiveness, and smart play to overpower the older Cuyahoga Falls players . . . and he was only getting started! The very next day, he went up against Cleveland Central Catholic and scored 21 points and grabbed 7 rebounds. The average senior scores fewer than ten points a game. LeBron was blowing that away as a 14-year-old freshman.

LeBron's skills were on display for the whole season. His team breezed past all their opponents. LeBron's averages of 18 points, 6.2 rebounds, and 3.6 assists were impressive. It helped the St. Vincent–St. Mary team go undefeated in LeBron's first season. For comparison, NBA legend, Kobe Bryant was a hyped freshman on a varsity team. He was also a starter, as well as the son of an NBA player. He averaged 18 points, just like LeBron, but Kobe had fewer rebounds and assists. Kobe led his team in scoring, but the team was lousy. They finished the season 4–20. LeBron led his team in scoring, rebounds, and assists, plus, LeBron's team never lost a game.

HIGH SCHOOL SUPERSTAR

Next up, the undefeated Fighting Irish headed to the playoffs. LeBron continued to use his skills to dominate his opponents. His coaches were impressed by his ability to play the game unselfishly. He played like a much older and wiser basketball player. He used his accurate passing to create easy scoring chances, which made everyone around him better. Most high school seniors get fewer than a few assists a game. LeBron averaged almost 5 assists in the playoffs as a freshman. No one had ever seen a freshman with such a complete game.

His coach, Keith Dambrot, called LeBron the perfect teammate. Dambrot loved how LeBron always got his teammates involved. He cared about more than scoring. LeBron went out of his way to pass the ball so his teammates could score too. Dambrot thought that sort of play showed incredible maturity for someone so young. His assistant coach, Steve Culp, felt the same way. Culp was sure LeBron could have put up 50 or more points a night if he wanted to, but LeBron did not care if he put up huge points in a loss. He was always concerned with winning. He knew the best way to win was to make his teammates better.

When LeBron wasn't making his teammates better with perfect passes, he used his height and weight

G.O.A.T. LEBRON JAMES

to overpower smaller players and gathered valuable rebounds. In one game, LeBron scored double digits in both rebounds and points (17 points, 11 rebounds). His first **double-double**! He enjoyed it so much, he managed his second double-double three games later in the semi-finals, scoring 19 points and 11 rebounds!

St. Vincent–St. Mary earned the right to play Jamestown's Greenview High School for the Ohio Division III championship. The game was the biggest of LeBron's life. They played at Value City Arena at Ohio State University in front of over 13,000 fans! That is more fans than the Cavaliers averaged the 2003 season. The gym was sold out. The spotlight didn't bother LeBron. He ended the game with 25 points, 9 rebounds, and 5 assists. Behind his huge performance, they won 73–55. The St. Vincent–St. Mary Fighting Irish finished the season 27–0. They were crowned Ohio's state champions, and LeBron was voted the playoffs' **Most Valuable Player**—an award no freshman had ever won before! It was his school's first championship since 1984, and it was all thanks to LeBron James. Instead of soaking up the spotlight, LeBron gave his MVP trophy to his friend and team captain, Maverick Carter. Maverick was the only senior on the team, and LeBron wanted him to have the award. Once again, he put a teammate before himself.

HIGH SCHOOL SUPERSTAR

MAVERICK CARTER

Maverick Carter and LeBron were teammates at St. Vincent–St. Mary. They are still teammates today, just not on the basketball court. Maverick is LeBron's business manager. He played basketball in college, but discovered his real passion while interning at Nike. He said the important thing he learned there is that marketing was all about telling stories. Nike "tells stories better than anyone in Hollywood." He wanted to help tell LeBron's story. When asked why he only represented LeBron, he said it was because LeBron is unique, one of a kind. Maverick manages LeBron's image, for better or for worse. He was the mastermind behind the Decision TV special. The special was considered a disaster for LeBron's public image. Many saw it as a selfish move and thought LeBron was turning his back on his teammates, fans, and hometown. On the flip side, Maverick pulled the strings to get LeBron in his first movie, *Trainwreck*, and manages LeBron's stake in European soccer club, F.C. Liverpool. Most recently, Maverick negotiated LeBron's sneaker deal with Nike. The deal is the largest in history. The actual dollar amount is secret, but when asked if it was a billion dollars, Maverick just pointed to the sky and said, "Higher."

G.O.A.T. LEBRON JAMES

The journalists at the game went nuts for LeBron. The media couldn't believe that the 6 foot 4 LeBron was only a 9th grader. Former Ohio state basketball star, Jay Burson, was impressed with how well LeBron knew what to do on the court in any situation. He was so calm and collected yet still aggressive. All the journalists agreed that his potential was limitless.

LeBron's own coach knew what kind of player LeBron could be. He knew most coaches would never get a chance to coach a player so talented. The rest of the country was starting to wake up to what everyone at St. Vincent–St. Mary already knew: LeBron was a once-in-a-generation player.

At the start of the 2000 season, LeBron wasted no time establishing himself as a force of nature. He opened the season with 23 points and in the very next game he scored 34 points and had 6 rebounds, 5 assists. It was his first time scoring over 30, and he would do it six more times that season. In one of those games, against Benedictine, LeBron had his first FORTY-point game. He shot 20 times and made 16 of those shots! It's hard enough to shoot that well in a gym, unguarded. But LeBron was doing it with everyone trying their hardest to make him miss. He was putting up amazing personal numbers, but he was excited about one thing only: the

HIGH SCHOOL SUPERSTAR

team started the season 9–0. LeBron had played 36 high school games without losing. He was unstoppable. But all streaks must end.

LeBron and his team's amazing run came to a halt when they played the number one team in the country, the Oak Hill Academy. Oak Hill was located in Virginia, so even though they never met in the state playoffs, they were one of St Vincent-St Mary's fiercest rivals. Oak Hill had future NBA superstar Carmelo Anthony on their roster, and they were famous for producing NBA talent. LeBron knew he would have to play well to beat such a good team. He also knew he had to make everyone on his team better. Inside, LeBron was nervous, but outside, he knew he had to lead. He felt intimidated by the talent on the other team. But Coach Culp told Lebron that they were good enough to win, and once LeBron bought in, everyone else on the team did, too. They followed his lead.

Every player on the Oak Hill roster was headed to a top-tier college on a basketball scholarship. Their center was 7 feet tall, something LeBron's team wasn't used to. LeBron and his team put up a strong fight. They tried their best and even led 52–42 at one point. But it wasn't enough. Oak Hill won 79–78 after LeBron barely missed a **buzzer beater**. Oak Hill Academy would become LeBron's greatest high school **rival**.

A RIVALRY BORN

A rivalry in sports is when two people or teams who compete for the same goal and are almost equal in skill. An example of a **rivalry** in the NBA is the one between the Lakers and the Celtics. LeBron has had a lot of rivalries in his long career, but Oak Hill Academy was his first big one.

LeBron and his team did not feel sorry for themselves or give up after the big loss. LeBron saw this loss as a reason to work even harder. The 15-year-old team leader told reporters that while he was disappointed, it was time to get back to work. The very next day he went right back to practice to try and make himself a better player. The team did not lose another game all season and reclaimed their throne as state champions! After two years in high school, LeBron's record was 53 and 1.

At the end of the season, LeBron took home a trunk load of awards. He was the playoffs MVP again. He was named Ohio All-State first team. He was the first sophomore ever to be named Ohio's Mr. Basketball, given to the state's best basketball player, a title he earned his junior and senior year, too. He was also named a USA Today All-American, something no one that young had ever done! He truly was one of a kind and was only going to get better.

HIGH SCHOOL SUPERSTAR

His junior year was a bit rockier with the Fighting Irish, but it was one of LeBron's best seasons. The team lost three regular season games, triple the number of his first two years combined! The team had a new coach and a harder schedule, but LeBron kept being LeBron. Over the season, he averaged 28 points, 9 rebounds, and 6 assists. He had twelve double-doubles, including a stretch in the playoffs where he had three in a row! He filled up scorecards and stadiums! So many people came to see LeBron that they had to move home games to the Rhodes Arena in Akron. But sold-out arenas were nothing compared to what happened next!

On February 18th, 2002, LeBron James, a high school junior from Akron, Ohio, was on the cover of *Sports Illustrated*. He is still, to this date, the only high school junior basketball player to be featured on the cover of the magazine. The cover was captioned, "the Chosen One," and would become one of the many nicknames that followed him through his career. At 16, LeBron wasn't just a basketball star, he was a media superstar. He was already used to NBA and college scouts watching every game, but now his every move was followed by thousands of fans, long before Twitter and Instagram.

Despite all the attention, and LeBron playing better than ever, his team lost the state Finals. In the loss,

G.O.A.T. LEBRON JAMES

LeBron again had a huge game. He played aggressively and used his speed to dance around defenders. When the defense tightened up under the basket, he drilled jumper after jumper. They did not have a way to stop him. By the end of the game, he had 32 points. He played so well that he still won the MVP. Even with the award, LeBron was heartbroken. He went right back to work to focus on getting better.

After the season was over, LeBron was again showered with awards. He was Ohio's Mr. Basketball again. Even more important, he was a rare junior NATIONAL Mr. Basketball. He was a USA Today All-American for the second time. There were also new awards, too. He was the Parade Player of the Year, and the Gatorade Player of the Year. He was the first junior ever to win these awards.

LeBron was so good that people thought he might skip his senior year of high school to go play in the NBA. There were no rules against it and it was clear LeBron, now standing at 6 foot 8, could compete with NBA talent. Even the athletic director of St. Vincent–St. Mary's agreed LeBron already played like a professional. But LeBron was a smart kid. He put those rumors to rest right away. He told the press first he had to finish school.

LeBron returned for the 2002–2003 season ready to take another shot at the championship, hoping to take his team to the Finals four years in a row. Things were tougher now, though. He not only had to focus on basketball, but he had to prepare for what happened after high school. It was clear he would be drafted in the NBA and almost certainly as the first overall pick. In the **NBA draft**, teams get to take turns picking new players, just like a captain chooses teammates on the playground. Everyone knew LeBron would get picked first.

Despite shoe sponsors, college recruiters, and NBA stars like Kobe Bryant and Michael Jordan now fighting for his attention, LeBron still improved his game. Remember how in LeBron's sophomore year, he scored more than 30 points in a game for the first time? In his senior year, he *averaged* more than 30 points a game. He scored more than 40 points five times and had two games where he scored more than *fifty points*! He had played in some high school games where entire teams weren't scoring fifty points, but LeBron did it all by himself not once, but twice!

NBA scouts said in LeBron's junior year that he was the number one pick if he decided to go. Those same scouts were blown away by how much his game had improved while he was still in school. He was already the best high school player his junior year, so to go continue growing during his senior year was an incredible feat! NBA scouts loved his **versatility**. He had a step back jumper, post moves, and was a great passer. It was amazing to see someone as big as LeBron who could do all of those things.

DID YOU KNOW?

In the off-season for basketball, many of the best players in the league play in camps such as the Five Star Camp. This camp has hosted the best of the best. Hall of Famers like Michael Jordan, Alonzo Mourning, Isiah Thomas, and current NBA superstars like Kevin Durant and Steph Curry all played at the Five Star Camp during their summers in high school. Despite how many talented players went through the camp, LeBron James was the only sophomore good enough to move up and play with the older guys. But LeBron, being LeBron, still wanted to play with his friends, so he struck a deal that let him play in both the freshman/sophomore games *and* the junior/senior games. He's the only player to ever play in both. Not surprisingly, he won each league and took home MVP honors for both. A scout at the camp said he had never seen a player as good as LeBron James.

Due to all this media attention, LeBron and St. Vincent–St. Mary's game against their rival Oak Hill Academy was the first ever prime-time nationally televised broadcast of a high school basketball game. The pressure was on for LeBron, now a senior, since he had never defeated Oak Hill. He was ready this time and played extremely well, all while being broadcast into homes all over the country. He scored 31 points, had 13 rebounds, and 6 assists, but, more importantly, he finally beat Oak Hill. After that, LeBron kept pouring it on for the rest of the season, playing the best high school basketball anyone had ever seen.

LeBron would propel his team to the Finals again for the fourth time in four years. They won behind a strong showing from LeBron. Three out of those four years, LeBron was the state champion. He won every award possible for a high school basketball player. He was the USA Today Player of the Year, Mr. Basketball, State Tournament MVP, Naismith Player of the Year, the Wootten Player of the Year, and the first ever Gatorade Athlete of the Year. Scouts called him a once-in-a-lifetime player. The local paper ran a daily column on him. His unique game—a combination of size, strength, and finesse—had captivated the nation. Fans, journalists, scouts, and his opponents all agreed: LeBron was the best high school player they had ever seen.

After his victory lap, LeBron still got to play a few more fun games, like the McDonalds All American High School Game. This game is an **exhibition game**, or just for fun, where the best high school seniors in the nation play each other. LeBron wasn't just facing other Ohio teams, he was now playing against America's best talent, all of them with college and professional basketball in their future. This was his second nationally televised game,

G.O.A.T. LEBRON JAMES

and more importantly, it was the last time scouts would see LeBron play a game before the draft. LeBron did not disappoint. He shredded the competition and walked away with another MVP award. Again, the scouts were impressed by LeBron's commitment to teamwork, preparation, determination, drive. One scout even noticed that LeBron was the first player on the court that day, warming up for the game.

Less than a month after his high school career came to a close in 2003, LeBron said what everyone already knew. He was going to skip college and go straight to the NBA. Scouts and members of the press predicted that he would be the first player picked to go to the NBA. Every team wanted to have him. He was the greatest high school player of all time and had potential to be an even greater NBA player. A month after he declared his intention to go to the NBA, the draft order was announced. The team with the first pick was none other than the Cleveland Cavaliers, his favorite team and the team of his home state. His NBA career would start less than an hour drive from where he and his mother once slept on couches. The boy who would later be called the King was going to stay home and build his NBA career right where he started his middle school and high school basketball careers, in Ohio.

3

WITNESS A GREAT START

The Cavs stunk. Fans knew it. The NBA knew it. LeBron knew it. Because of how the **NBA Draft** works, the worst teams get the first picks of incoming players. The Cavaliers had only won 17 games the previous year, and they had lost 50 or more out of 82 games the past four years in a row. They didn't just have one bad season; they had many. They had stunk for a long time. But many fans in Cleveland and the rest of Ohio had faith that the hometown hero could turn around the dismal franchise.

Before LeBron even set foot in a Cavaliers gym, he was already a multimillionaire. In 2003, LeBron signed a record-setting, seven-year, $90 million deal with Nike. It was the largest endorsement deal ever signed by a rookie. For comparison, Michael Jordan's Nike deal

G.O.A.T. LEBRON JAMES

LeBron scoring against the Spurs

when he was a rookie was only $2.5 million. Jordan's deal was huge at the time, but it was nothing compared to LeBron's.

ENDORSEMENTS

LeBron James Endorsements (2018):
- NIKE
- VERIZON
- INTEL
- COCA-COLA
- BEATS BY DRE
- KIA

In 2017 LeBron made $86 million, and only $30 million of that was from his league-high basketball salary. He made another $56 million from companies paying him to advertise their products. Nike has paid him more a billion dollars for a lifelong endorsement deal. He makes more in endorsement deals than any other active American athlete. (He is second in the world behind tennis star player Roger Federer.)

WITNESS A GREAT START

Financially, LeBron had already made it. He had enough money for his mom and him to live lavish lifestyles for the rest of their lives. Even if his game got worse over time, he was set. But LeBron was a champion and wanted to win for winning's-sake, not just for the money. He had a tough road ahead, since the Cavs were a mess. Some players didn't believe LeBron would be able to turn the team around. After all, he was just a kid fresh out of high school, playing against men in their 20s and 30s who had been in the NBA for years. The starting power forward for the Cavs, Carlos Boozer, thought they had better players at LeBron's position. LeBron, at 6 foot 8 and 225 pounds, was still playing shooting guard, but he would eventually switch to small forward. Boozer had no idea what the kid from Akron would become. The most critical teammate was Darius Miles, another **prep-to-pro** (high school to NBA) player. Miles was vocal about how he did not think it was possible for a high school player to turn around an NBA team.

They were right to be a bit nervous about a high school to pro player. So many prep-to-pro players before him had been busts, only lasting a few years in the league. It was a huge gamble by the Cavaliers to put so much faith in a player this young. Only time would tell if LeBron could handle the leap from playing 17- and 18-year-olds to playing NBA professionals.

G.O.A.T. LEBRON JAMES

LeBron did not make the fans wait long to see what he was capable of. His very first NBA game was October 29, 2003. Six months earlier, he was a high school senior and now, he was starting in an NBA game against the Sacramento Kings. His team was a collection of young players and NBA **journeymen**, or guys who play for many teams over their careers. The Sacramento Kings had NBA stars Mike Bibby, Vlade Divac, and 3-time NBA All Star Peja Stojakovic. The Kings had won 59 games and gone to the Western Conference Finals the year before. Meanwhile, the Cavs had lost 65 games and had the league's worst record. This meant that LeBron did not have time to ease into the NBA. He played against one of the best teams, right out of the gate.

And he dazzled the crowd! In his first ten minutes on the court, he had 9 points and looked even better than he had in high school. He was grabbing rebounds, making amazing passes that set his teammates up for baskets, and scoring in every way. Late in the 1st quarter, he jumped into a passing lane and stole the ball. He gathered the ball and sprinted for the basket. Just like when he played his middle school teachers, no one was in his way. He sprinted from half court and when he got to the free throw line, he lifted off, soar-

WITNESS A GREAT START

ing to the hoop with the ball pulled way back behind his head, and slammed it into the hoop with force and confidence. It was as if he screamed to all his fans, "I'm here!"

LeBron ended the game with 25 points, the most ever scored by a player right out of high school in his first game. He scored easily on NBA defenders, and he was only 18 years old. His critics were stunned and his supporters were excited. After the game, LeBron was only concerned with one stat: the L. The Cavs lost 106 to 92. Just as in high school, LeBron didn't care about his stats if his team didn't win. Even though he set records with his opening performance, his team was now 0–1. LeBron wasn't happy. He told reporters that he felt like he could have done more for his team.

The Cavaliers would lose 5 more games before LeBron could experience his first NBA team victory against the Washington Wizards, 111–98. Eventually, the Cavs won a few more games, but the team was struggling over all. LeBron played well, but it wasn't enough to raise the team to super-star status.

LeBron knew, even at 18, he had to be a leader again, just like he was in high school. The team needed a point guard to succeed. The **point guard** is the primary ball handler and runs the offense. LeBron jumped at the chance to make his team better. Most teams would not feel comfortable coordinating the offense through an 18-year-old, but LeBron was special. He spent day and night learning the offense, and his coach, Paul Silas, was amazed at how quickly he picked it up—faster than any of the other players on the team. LeBron knew as point guard he could get the other players involved. He didn't just learn his role in the offense, he learned every single position. This way he could understand what player was doing and where to get them the ball. He would rather get highlight dunks and big shots for his teammates than for himself.

The team gradually started improving with LeBron at point guard. Many of the team's players began to warm up to the young prodigy. After all, he was crushing it at a position he had never played before and was making everyone around him better. Yet some players were not so convinced. The team's top scorer from the year before, Ricky Davis, wasn't impressed. He would throw parties but leave young LeBron out. He also berated LeBron on the court for not passing to him. Ricky had been a 20-point scorer the previous season and insisted the Cavs were still his team. He wanted to take as many shots as possible and LeBron spreading the ball around made that harder. Eventu-

WITNESS A GREAT START

ally, the coaching staff had enough of Davis trying to push around LeBron. He was traded not long after for two veteran players who might not have been stars like Davis, but played the kind of team basketball Silas was looking for. After the trade, the team played more unselfishly. They even had a seven-game winning streak. For a team that only won 17 games the year before, this was a huge deal. Almost as important as their win streak was the fact that LeBron was starting to make friends on the team. He was starting to feel like he belonged.

LeBron continued to surprise even his biggest supporters by posting huge numbers. On March 27, 2004, LeBron became the youngest player in NBA history to score 40 points or more in a game against the New Jersey Nets, in a 107–103 victory. He also had 12 games throughout the season where he scored more than 30 points. This was absolutely unheard of for a rookie, not to mention one who was only 18 years old.

Everyone thought the team would be better with LeBron, but no one imagined how quickly that would happen. They finished the season with a record of 35–47. It was a losing season, meaning that the team lost more games than it won, but it would be the last losing season of LeBron's NBA career.

G.O.A.T. LEBRON JAMES

CONFERENCES

The NBA is divided into two conferences: East and West. Those conferences have three divisions each. At the end of the season, the top eight teams in each conference go to the playoffs.

WESTERN CONFERENCE

NORTHWEST DIVISION: Denver Nuggets, Minnesota Timberwolves, Oklahoma City Thunder, Portland Trailblazers, Utah Jazz

PACIFIC DIVISION: Golden State Warriors, Los Angeles Clippers, Los Angeles Lakers, Phoenix Suns, Sacramento Kings

SOUTHWEST DIVISION: Dallas Mavericks, Houston Rockets, Memphis Grizzlies, Memphis Grizzlies, New Orleans Pelicans, San Antonio Spurs

EASTERN CONFERENCE

ATLANTIC: Boston Celtics, Brooklyn Nets, New York Knicks, Philadelphia 76ers, Toronto Raptors

CENTRAL DIVISION: Chicago Bulls, Cleveland Cavaliers, Detroit Pistons, Indiana Pacers, Milwaukee Bucks

SOUTHEAST DIVISION: Atlanta Hawks, Charlotte Hornets, Miami Heat, Orlando Magic, Washington Wizards

WITNESS A GREAT START

Despite the losing record, the season was not all negative. Throughout the season, the NBA gives out a Rookie of the Month award for each conference. LeBron James won it every single month for the Eastern Conference. Considering this, it should be no surprise that LeBron also took home the Rookie of the Year award. He was only the second player to win the award coming straight from high school, after Amar'e Stoudemire, who won it the year before. Everyone else who won had played in college first.

• • •

A BATTLE OF ROOKIES

LeBron's rookie season was dominant. He averaged 20.9 points, 5.5 rebounds, and 5.9 assists. He is the first and only prep-to-pro player to average a 20/5/5 line. Compare those to other superstar players from around the same time: Steph Curry (18/4/6) and Kevin Durant (20/4/2). Both played in college before the NBA but still were not as good as LeBron. Another prep to pro star, Kobe Bryant (8/1/2), didn't even come close. It's clear that LeBron played one of the best rookie seasons ever. As far as prep-to-pro, LeBron is the G.O.A.T. He was only 19 years old and already one of the best players in the league.

LEBRON JAMES
POINTS: 20.9
REBOUNDS: 5.5
ASSISTS: 5.9
STEALS: 1.6
BLOCKS: .7
AWARDS: ROOKIE OF THE YEAR, ALL-ROOKIE FIRST TEAM

WITNESS A GREAT START

KOBE BRYANT
POINTS: 7.6
REBOUNDS: 1.9
ASSISTS: 1.3
STEALS: .7
BLOCKS: .3
AWARDS: ALL-ROOKIE SECOND TEAM

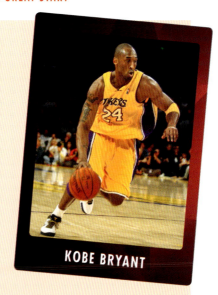

KOBE BRYANT

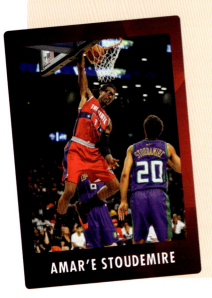

AMAR'E STOUDEMIRE

AMAR'E STOUDEMIRE
POINTS: 13.5
REBOUNDS: 8.8
ASSISTS: 1.0
STEALS: .8
BLOCKS: 1.1.
AWARDS: ROOKIE OF THE YEAR, ALL-ROOKIE FIRST TEAM

G.O.A.T. LEBRON JAMES

Despite all the praise and awards, LeBron was unhappy. Fueled by the first losing season of his life, he came back determined to improve as a team. Everything LeBron did, he did to win more games. He didn't care about personal records or awards and the magazine covers. He had his eye on winning. This drive to be great is one of LeBron's most important traits.

His sophomore season had some ups and downs. The team got along better than the previous year and LeBron was the undisputed leader. But there was also a losing streak that ended with Coach Silas being fired. Despite this, LeBron continued to improve. He upped his averages in every single statistic and the team posted its first winning record in five years! They ended the season 42 wins and 40 losses. LeBron averaged an eye-popping 27.2 points per game with 7.4 rebounds and 7.2 assists.

One of the things LeBron James would become known for is the triple-double. A triple-double is like a double-double but instead of scoring double digits in two statistical categories, you score double digits in three. The most common triple-double includes double digits in points, rebounds, and assists. In his second season, LeBron recorded his first triple-double. On January 19, 2005, LeBron finally achieved one

WITNESS A GREAT START

of the most difficult statistical feats in basketball, when he scored 27 points, grabbed 11 rebounds, and passed for 10 assists in a win against the Portland Trailblazers. At 20, he was the youngest to ever achieve this feat. He did it again two games later against the Golden State Warriors on January 22, when the Cavaliers defeated the Warriors 105–87. He had 28 points, 12 rebounds, and 10 assists. He ended the season with 4 triple-doubles total. Not long after, LeBron reached another landmark. In March 2005, he scored 56 points against the Toronto Raptors, making him the youngest player to ever score that much in an NBA game. By the end of the season, he had 5 games over 40 points and 25 double-doubles. He was also the youngest player to score 2,000 total points in the NBA. With these numbers, it was no surprise that LeBron was selected to play in the All-Star Game. He's been chosen to play every year since.

THE NBA ALL-STAR GAME

The NBA takes a break every year at the halfway point of the season. During this break, they play the All-Star Game. All the best players from the NBA form two teams and play each other in an exhibition game. Being selected to an All-Star team means a player is one of the best of the NBA. The first All Star game was

G.O.A.T. LEBRON JAMES

played all the way back in 1951 and drew almost 10,000 people. It grew from there and in 2010 it set a record for most attendees at a basketball game with 108,713 people. All-Star Weekend has turned into a celebration of all things NBA, including a dunk contest, a skills contest, and a celebrity basketball game.

In just two seasons, LeBron had developed into one of the best players in the NBA. He was respected by fans and even his NBA peers were realizing he was more than just hype—he had proven himself to be hands down the best player on his team. Still, LeBron wanted more. He wanted to make the playoffs and win the NBA championship.

4

POSTSEASON LEBRON

Two years. That is all it took for young LeBron James to turn around the worst team in the league. By 2005, the once forgotten Cavaliers were filling their stadium with fans, and LeBron's jersey was the best-selling in the league. King James was becoming the most famous Cavalier of all time.

LeBron, now 20, went into the 2005–2006 season more focused than ever. The Cavaliers management was also focused. They made a big splash by courting star free agent, Larry Hughes, who had just come off his best season of his career. He led the Washington Wizards to their first playoff appearance in eight years. Larry gave LeBron a true second scoring option and was an excellent defender. Larry was voted All NBA Defense the year before. Most important, unlike Davis during LeBron's rookie year, Larry knew he was brought in to help LeBron, not the other way around. It

G.O.A.T. LEBRON JAMES

TRADES AND FREE AGENCY

It always seems like NBA players keep moving to new teams. That's because a lot of them are! The two main ways players go to a new team is by trade or free agency. A **trade** is when two teams agree to swap players or draft picks. For example, if a team need a point guard but already has a couple shooting guards, they might find a team that needs shooting guards but has a point guard they don't want. Trades can get really complicated and involve 3 or even more teams!

The other way players switch teams is **free agency.** Every player signs a contract with a team. Those contracts say the player will stay with the team for a certain amount of years. Once that time is up, they can sign a new contract or enter free agency. In free agency, any team can sign a player to a contract. LeBron switched teams when he was a free agent three times!

was LeBron's team and Hughes was excited to help whatever way he could. Partly thanks to Hughes and the rest of the Cavalier supporting cast, LeBron's season was one of highlight dunks, fancy passes, and full box scores.

With amazing numbers, LeBron was named to his second All-Star team. He became the youngest player ever to win the All-Star Most Valuable Player award when he scored 29 points to help the Eastern conference win 122–120. On top of all that, LeBron's historic regular season led to him coming in second place for Most Valuable Player Award, which is given every year to the league's best player and is the NBA's highest individual honor. At

POSTSEASON LEBRON

21, he received more MVP votes than NBA superstars like Dirk Nowitzki and Kobe Bryant that year.

LEBRON AT 21—IN NUMBERS

2005–2006 SEASON AVERAGES

Points: 31.4 (career high)   **Rebounds:** 7   **Double-doubles:** 21

Assists: 6.6   **Triple-doubles:** 5

4th player in history to average 30 points, 7 rebounds, 6 assists. Youngest player to ever reach 4,000 career points.

LeBron's regular season was incredible, but the fun was just beginning. The Cavaliers, once a laughingstock of the NBA, were heading to the playoffs after finishing with a 50–32 record. Remember, this was only a few years after winning only 17 games. They matched up with the Washington Wizards for the LeBron's first ever playoff series.

LeBron James had never played on a stage this big. He had also never been so nervous before a game. When he entered the Cleveland arena, it was filled to capacity. The 20,562 fans were buzzing. They waved white towels and wore black T-shirts that said "Witness" on them. Seeing so many people believe in him made LeBron a little less nervous, but he still had some jitters. LeBron made his way to the scorer's table to perform his pregame ritual: the chalk toss. Before every game, LeBron filled his hands with chalk and tossed it in the air to signal the start of the game. It was always a fan favorite and this time was no different. The crowd exploded with excitement. It was time to get to work.

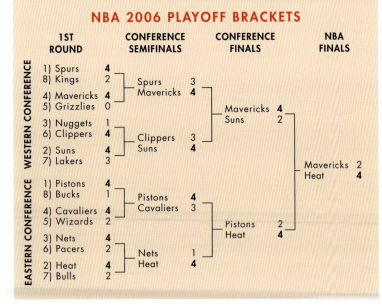

PLAYOFFS

At the end of every regular season, the eight teams from the Western and Eastern conferences with the best records advance to the NBA Playoffs. In the playoffs, teams face off in best of seven game series. The winner of the series advances. The losers' season is over. There are 4 rounds to the playoffs (divisional, conference semi-finals, conference finals, and NBA Finals) until there is only one team left. That team is crowned the NBA Champions.

NBA 2006 PLAYOFF BRACKETS

WESTERN CONFERENCE

1ST ROUND:
- 1) Spurs 4
- 8) Kings 2
- 4) Mavericks 4
- 5) Grizzlies 0
- 3) Nuggets 1
- 6) Clippers 4
- 2) Suns 4
- 7) Lakers 3

CONFERENCE SEMIFINALS:
- Spurs 3
- Mavericks 4
- Clippers 3
- Suns 4

CONFERENCE FINALS:
- Mavericks 4
- Suns 2

EASTERN CONFERENCE

1ST ROUND:
- 1) Pistons 4
- 8) Bucks 1
- 4) Cavaliers 4
- 5) Wizards 2
- 3) Nets 4
- 6) Pacers 2
- 2) Heat 4
- 7) Bulls 2

CONFERENCE SEMIFINALS:
- Pistons 4
- Cavaliers 3
- Nets 1
- Heat 4

CONFERENCE FINALS:
- Pistons 2
- Heat 4

NBA FINALS:
- Mavericks 2
- Heat 4

POSTSEASON LEBRON

LeBron started the game slow. He was nervous and wanted to wait for just the right shot. He passed to teammates and moved the ball around. On such a big stage, it seemed as if he was having trouble finding his focus. What if he choked? What if he let everyone down? Finally, almost three minutes into the game, LeBron dribbled up to the 3-point line and fired off a shot. It hung in the air and then came back down, completely missing the rim. Airball! LeBron's first shot in an NBA playoff game was a whiff, but LeBron didn't have time to think about it. He hustled back to get on defense. Caron Butler of the Wizards attempted a driving layup, but missed. LeBron leapt up and pulled down the rebound. He led the offense to the other end. It did not take long for LeBron to forget about his bad first shot. LeBron drove to the basket from the 3-point line. He beat his man and rolled in for an easy layup. His first playoff basket! All the nervousness washed away. It was just another game.

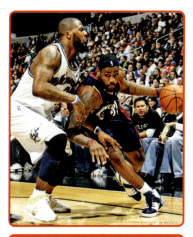

Lebron making a move against the Washington Wizards

Once he realized that, he didn't let up. And LeBron wasn't just scoring. He made dazzling passes to his open teammates and ripped down rebounds. After his slow start, LeBron ended the game with 11 rebounds and 11 assists to go with 32 points. He had a triple double in his first ever playoff game! The most important stat to LeBron? The W. The win made up for all of it. The airball, the nervousness, the huge expectations. He overcame them. The Cavaliers went on to win the series 4 to 2.

LeBron and the Cavaliers dropped the first two games of the next series to the heavily favored Pistons. The Pistons were a basketball powerhouse and the Cavaliers took them to the brink. But despite the 3-win streak that they had in the middle, the Cavaliers ultimately lost the playoff series. The loss in game 7 stung since they had squandered a 3–2 series lead. It was a disappointing end to a great season, but everyone knew it would not be the last trip to the playoffs for the Cavaliers. The most important thing they learned was that they could handle it. LeBron and his teammates could compete with the best teams on the biggest stage.

The very next season (2006–2007), LeBron and his team came back and did it all over again, winning 50 games on their way to another playoff appearance. LeBron was devastated by the loss to the Pistons, especially since they were only one game away from winning the series. LeBron focused his disappointment and energy on improving the areas of his game that he knew were imperfect. He hired a shooting coach and would stay after practice, sometimes for hours, practicing his outside shot. LeBron knew the reason the Pistons had succeeded the year before was because of their intense defense. He wanted to add that to his game. He placed a new focus and energy on defense and used his athleticism to shut down teams' best players and protect the rim with big blocks. Even while he was being called one of the best basketball players in the world, LeBron kept working on his game.

The Cavaliers management wanted to improve as a team, too. They brought in new players to help LeBron on the court, but had trouble attracting stars. LeBron didn't want to be a one-man show in a game that required 5 players. Larry Hughes continued to deliver for LeBron as a good second option, but the team was not able to attract a third star to complete the team. The Cavaliers continued to rely on crafty veterans, which was good enough for LeBron at the time, but left them with depth problems.

As fate would have it, LeBron's Cavs played the Washington Wizards in the first round of the 2007 playoffs. The previous season, the Wizards won two games in the series, but this year was different. LeBron had leveled up, becoming an even better player. In the series, he averaged almost 28 points with more than 8 rebounds and 7 assists. The Cavaliers easily swept the Wizards. A **sweep** in the playoffs is when a team wins the series without losing a single game.

After Washington, they played a much tougher series against the New Jersey Nets, but still won the second round 4-2. This meant that they had made it to the Eastern Conference Finals, a first for LeBron and only the third time for the Cleveland Cavaliers. The Eastern Conference Finals matches up the best two teams in the East, so it was no surprise that their competition was fierce. The Cavs would be playing none other than the Detroit Pistons, the same team that beat them in the playoffs the year before.

The Cavs lost the first two games of the series in Detroit to a Pistons team that was playing near-perfect basketball. LeBron was hounded by the Pistons trademark impassable defense. But in game 3, the Cavs got to play on their home turf, where they seemed to lock in to a rhythm. LeBron fired off 32 points in game 3 and dished out 11 assists in game 4. LeBron was a human highlight reel for these two games, but no highlight would be shown more than his rim-rocking dunk over Pistons star center Rasheed Wallace.

POSTSEASON LEBRON

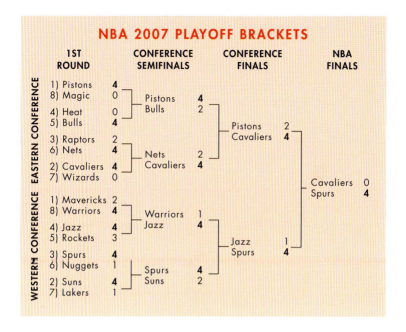

After winning both home games, the Cavaliers were headed back to Detroit. There is an old saying in basketball: "It isn't a series until someone loses at home." So far, both teams had defended their home court, tying the series at 2–2. In game 5, LeBron was determined to attack the legendary Pistons defense. He told his teammates before the game that the only way to beat their defense was to be aggressive for the entire game. At points, LeBron drove hard to the basket and made it look easy. He started from behind the 3-point line and dribbled smoothly around three defenders. He wove and drove. He went over the defense.

He went around the defense, and when he had to, he went *through* the defense. He hit shots inside and out. No matter what defenses or **double teams**, when two players defend one player, the Pistons threw at him, LeBron would either get by them or pass to an open teammate. While LeBron had his way with their defense, the Pistons offense continued to deliver. For every point LeBron scored, the Pistons answered. This pushed LeBron even harder. He was determined to use every ounce of energy he had. With three minutes left, the Pistons pulled ahead by 7 points. LeBron immediately answered with a layup, a 3-pointer, and a thunderous dunk to bring it back to a tie with only 9 seconds left. The 4th quarter ended with it knotted up at 91.

After a short rest, LeBron somehow found even more energy to help his team and to keep punishing the Pistons defense, but the Pistons offense kept coming back. The first overtime ended with the score tied at 100. In the second overtime, the game was still tied, 107 to 107. LeBron had the ball and was matched up against Chauncy Billups, the scrappy Detroit point guard. LeBron drove and got a step on Billups. Billups couldn't recover and the rest of the defense did not react fast enough. LeBron gathered the ball, took two huge steps, and leapt to the basket. The clock showed less than three seconds left. Three Piston defenders jumped toward LeBron as he cast up the shot.

POSTSEASON LEBRON

The ball lightly bounced off the backboard and into the hoop. A textbook layup. With 2.2 seconds left, LeBron had put his team up 109–107 with the first shot he learned to shoot. The Pistons were unable to answer and the game was over. Cavs won. LeBron limped back to the sidelines and collapsed into a chair. He had spent every last bit of strength he had. So much so, he did not realize he had scored every single Cavalier point in both overtimes. LeBron was not concerned about his incredible 48 points. He just wanted to go home and rest up for the next game.

The memory of the defeat from the previous season was still fresh for LeBron, and he was determined not to repeat it. The next game was in Cleveland after a day of rest. LeBron badly needed it and came back to the Cleveland arena with fresh legs. The game was back and forth for the first 3 quarters. The Cavs went into the 4th quarter up by one point, but they jumped out on a long scoring run, and the Pistons had problems scoring. The home team Cavaliers outscored the Pistons by 15 points in the 4th quarter. When the final buzzer rang, it didn't quite seem real. At 22 years old, the kid from Akron was on his way to his first NBA Finals.

The Cavaliers met the San Antonio Spurs in the NBA finals. The Spurs team practiced shut down defense and slow paced half-court offense. Their coach, Gregg Popovich,

G.O.A.T. LEBRON JAMES

was known as an expert tactician. LeBron knew going in that Popovich had a plan to shut him down. LeBron went in confident that he could handle their defense just like he had handled the Pistons defense. The Spurs not only had one of the greatest coaches out there, they had experience. The Spurs players had played in 103 NBA finals games between them. On the Cavaliers, only one player had ever been to the NBA Finals. The Spurs were the heavy favorite.

LeBron's confidence quickly evaporated after game 1. Playing in San Antonio, the Spurs assigned Bruce Bowen to defend James. Bowen pestered and harassed LeBron all game. If LeBron got around one guy, there was another Spurs player there to stop him. Their team defense completely shut down LeBron. He turned the ball over six times and only scored 14 points. LeBron knew he had to play better to win and he vowed to his teammates he would. But game 2 was more of the same. LeBron's confidence was gone. He had climbed to the biggest stage in the NBA and was failing.

LeBron never did figure out the Spurs defense. The Cavaliers lost in four games. They were on the bad end of a sweep. LeBron stood on the sidelines and watched as the Spurs celebrated their 4th Larry O'Brien trophy, the championship trophy awarded to the winner of the Finals, in 9 years. He couldn't take it. He turned his back to the celebration and headed for the locker room.

54

5

MOST VALUABLE LEBRON

The defeat by San Antonio stuck with LeBron. The sweetness from beating the Cavs' rival Detroit Pistons was gone and all that remained was the bitterness of defeat. LeBron didn't blame his teammates or coaches for the sweep. He placed the responsibility solely on his own shoulders. It was clear to him that he had to be ten times better if he wanted to be a champion. If LeBron got better, it would all trickle down to his teammates. When he played well, the team played well. In San Antonio, he turned the ball over and shot poorly and that took opportunities away from his team. After the loss, San Antonio Spurs star center Tim Duncan told LeBron that soon the league would belong to LeBron. That was little consolation for LeBron—he did not want to wait, so he got to work.

G.O.A.T. LEBRON JAMES

During the next season, on February 27, 2008, he became the youngest player to ever score 10,000 points in his career, and was once again an All-Star. He even passed Brad Daugherty as the Cavaliers all-time leading scorer. He was still only 23 years old. That year he won the NBA scoring title by averaging more points in the season than any other player. They Cavaliers still fell short of LeBron's goal: another NBA Finals.

Before the start of the 2008–2009 season, the Cavaliers traded for hotshot point guard Mo Williams. The Cavs were starting to get nervous that LeBron would leave them and go to another team. The arrival of Mo took pressure off LeBron, much like the arrival of Larry Hughes had seasons earlier. Teams could no longer double-team or triple-team him on every play. LeBron was unleashed. The difference was Mo was a point guard. He could run the offense for LeBron to give the defense a different look if something wasn't working. Instead of bringing the ball up court every play, LeBron could play off the ball to get into scoring position. Mo, like LeBron, was an excellent passer and was able to get LeBron the ball right where he needed it to score. The change let LeBron open up his game, and he improved in almost every single statistic. LeBron became the all-time leader for the Cavaliers in rebounds, steals, and free throws that sea-

MOST VALUABLE LEBRON

son. The 2008–2009 Cavaliers hit a Cavaliers record with 66 wins, the most regular-season wins of any team that season. They only lost 16 times all year!

The Cavaliers were the best regular season team, and LeBron put up some of the best numbers of his career. It was no surprise that when the media voted on the league's Most Valuable Player, LeB-

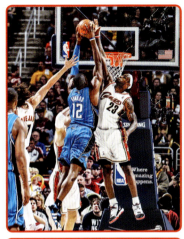

LeBron blocking Dwight Howard of the Orlando Magic

ron James ran away with the award. That is what happens when you average 28–7–7 and lead your team to an astounding 66 wins. Not only did he make the offense click, he was also the anchor of a league-leading defense. LeBron came in second for Defensive Player of the Year voting behind Orlando Magic's Dwight Howard. A player that dominant at both ends of the ball is a shoe-in for the MVP award.

When LeBron told the NBA he wanted to have his MVP ceremony at "home," they assumed he meant the Quicken Loans Arena in Cleveland, where LeBron had led the Cavaliers to a 39–2 home record. But when LeBron said home, he meant the gym where he learned to become a

G.O.A.T. LEBRON JAMES

great basketball player and person. LeBron James wanted to receive his first MVP award in the gym of St Vincent-St Mary, where his dream of becoming an NBA player began.

On May 4, 2009, LeBron drove himself to the MVP ceremony. He took the long way. He drove past the houses and apartments where he used to live on couches and missed dozens of days of school. He drove by the dirt yards where he would play football with his friends. He was flooded with memories of how he grew up and how different things were. Fifteen years after LeBron and his mom were bouncing from home to home, he drove by in a luxury car on his way to receive an award for being the best player in the NBA.

LeBron arrived at the St Vincent-St Mary gym in downtown Akron and he was nervous again. He was not speaking in front of the capacity Quicken Loans Arena like the NBA planned, but a small crowd consisting of students and teachers at St Vincent-St Mary, along with his teammates, coaches, family, and friends. When he took the podium in the gym he played in just six years earlier, the crowd began to chant, "MVP! MVP! MVP!" LeBron held a clenched fist to his mouth and fought back tears. He waited for the chants to die down and for his tears to go away before he spoke.

LeBron started by thanking the greats that came

MOST VALUABLE LEBRON

before him. Magic Johnson, Kareem, Oscar Robertson. All giants on whose shoulders he stood to become the player he was. He thanked his teammates, whose hard work allowed him to be there to begin with. He pointed out that those 14 guys put in the work so he could be MVP. He thanked everyone who believed in him: Frankie Walker, Dru Joyce, Coach Dambrot, and his proud mother, Gloria. Then he spoke to the students in the audience. He wanted one thing to be clear: hard work pays off. He once played in that gym; that's where it had all begun. Dreams can come true. LeBron held the award tight and walked away from the podium, once again fighting back tears. He never forgot where he came from and he wanted those students to never forget where they could go.

MVP VOTING

The NBA Most Valuable Player award is given every year to the best player in the NBA. But who decides who is the best player in the NBA? It is put to a vote! 100 members of the press who do not work for any NBA teams get to vote. The votes are secret so press members can vote for whoever they think is the best without fans or players getting mad at them. Each journalist votes for their top five players. Each 1st place vote gets 10 points, 2nd place is 7 points, 3rd is 5 points, 4th is 3 points, and 5th is 1 point. Whichever player has the most points is the award winner! There is rarely total agreement among all journalists, but it is often close, like when LeBron got all but one MVP 1st place vote in 2010.

The very next year, on May 2, 2010, LeBron won the MVP again with even more astounding stats: 29.7 points, 7.3 rebounds, and 8.6 assists per game. LeBron was the best player in the NBA two years in a row. The second one was not any less sweet. He decided to receive the second award in the gym for the University of Akron, where Coach Dambrot coached and where LeBron played games after the crowds grew too big for the high school gym. He once again held the ceremony in his hometown to remind the crowd, and himself, that he's just a kid from Akron. Standing with him to accept the Most Valuable Player award were his girlfriend, his two sons, and his mother.

By this point, there was a lot of speculation about whether LeBron would stay with the Cavaliers at the end of the year. His contract was up and he was a free agent. He could play for any team in the NBA. He knew the questions were swirling in the minds of all of those in attendance. He wanted to reassure them, but he did not even know what his decision would be. He knew that everything he did, he did not just do for himself. Every win was a win for Cleveland, Akron, and all of Northeast Ohio. He wanted to remain loyal to them, but he also had a drive to win. His team had not been back to the Finals since Tim Duncan and the Spurs swept them. The loss still stung and the only way to relieve it was to go back to the Finals. On stage accepting his second MVP award, LeBron looked out to the crowd and thought about Ohio. He realized even if he left Ohio, he would still just be a little kid from Akron.

The Cavs and LeBron were poised to make a deep run into the playoffs with their best supporting cast yet and LeBron was playing his best season. The press and the fans were sure this would be the year that King James finally took his throne as an NBA champion. But 11 days after accepting his second consecutive MVP, LeBron and the Cavaliers fell short again. After rolling over the Chicago Bulls in the first round, the Cavaliers fell apart. They lost to the Boston Celtics in six games. The Celtics,

LeBron on the Cavs against the Celtics' Paul Pierce and Kevin Garnett

just like the Spurs and all the other teams that beat him, had three superstars on their team. They showed the world that three stars were better than one player, even if he was the best in the league. The Cavaliers lost by an average of 17 points a game. Even with spectacular play from LeBron (who averaged 26 points, 9 rebounds, and 7 assists per game), the team got beaten on both ends of the floor. Another promising regular season felt wasted.

When the game was over, LeBron heard something he had not heard in the Quicken Loans Arena, at least not directed at him. He heard boos. This hurt deep down because not only had LeBron given the first seven years of his career to the city, but this was his home. In the moment, he did not know what to do. He had plenty of individual achievements to show for it (2 MVPs, 6 All-Star selections, 6 All NBA teams, 2 All Defense teams, Rookie of the Year), but there was one award that he had not gotten—an NBA championship. He looked up to the stands and then started walking to the tunnel out of the arena. As he left, he untucked his Cavaliers jersey. He took a few more steps, took the Cleveland #23 jersey off, and walked out of Quicken Loans arena.

6

TAKING HIS TALENTS TO SOUTH BEACH

After leaving the Cleveland arena, LeBron knew he had to make the toughest decision of his career. Would he stay in Cleveland and keep trying to win all by himself? Or would he find a new team that was better prepared to win an NBA championship? No one, including LeBron, knew what he was going to decide. Still, it was something he had been thinking about for years.

Let's go back in time two years from this point. It was 2008 and LeBron was on the other side of the globe in Beijing, China. He was representing the United States in the Olympics. At his first Olympics, in 2004, the USA won the bronze medal. But because the USA had so much talent, it was seen as a disappointment. In his second Olympics, people called the 2008 squad the "Redeem Team." They were trying to redeem their 2004 performance. While playing on the Redeem Team, LeBron became close friends with Dwyane Wade and Chris Bosh.

Dwyane and Chris were incredible talents who had played with LeBron before, but Beijing is where they really clicked. The three stars played great basketball. Dwyane scored an average of 16 points per game. Chris led the team in rebounds with an average of 9 points per game. And, of course, LeBron, the ultimate teammate, led in assists, with an average of 5.6 per game. They were winning games by huge margins and having tons of fun doing it.

The team ended up going undefeated. The Finals were against Spain, a team with several NBA players as well, but Team USA beat them with ease. Dwyane scored an amazing 27 points, and LeBron backed him up with 14 points, 6 rebounds, and 3 assists. The big story wasn't the team's offense, though. The Americans used their size and athleticism to play machine-like team defense. They held their opponents to 39% shooting through the tournament. LeBron was awarded his first Olympic gold medal, one of the highest honors for any athlete.

In Beijing, LeBron was really having fun playing basketball. He, Dwyane, and Chris had skills that complemented each other's games. LeBron loved being able to focus on passing the ball and playing tough defense. Even though he was a gifted scorer, it took a lot out of him to always have to carry his teammates. Though the three friends have never publicly admitted it, many in the press think that it was in Beijing that LeBron, Dwyane, and Chris decided to do whatever they could to play on the same NBA team.

Back to 2010. LeBron's contract was up. His team failed to reach the Finals again despite his winning the MVP for the second year in a row. It was a tough choice. Should he stay with the team that picked him? Or should he go to a new city and play with his friends?

LeBron playing for Team USA during the Oylmpics

A few days before LeBron gave his decision, Chris Bosh announced that he would join the Miami Heat.

LeBron agonized over his decision on whether to stay with Cleveland or go to another team that would give him a better chance to win a title. On July 8, 2010 during a live cable television special, LeBron announced his plan for the next season. The show was called *The Decision*. Nearly 10 million people tuned in to watch.

LeBron made his announcement by saying the now famous sentence, "In the fall, I'm taking my talents to

G.O.A.T. LEBRON JAMES

LeBron on the Heat

South Beach." By South Beach, he was referring to the South Beach neighborhood in Miami, Florida. He was leaving Cleveland to join Chris Bosh and Dwyane Wade on the Miami Heat. Fans in Miami were excited, while fans in LeBron's hometown were heartbroken. They felt betrayed and some even burned his jersey. The Cleveland Cavaliers were dumbstruck. Many fans saw it as egotistical and selfish. He was panned by media, even outside of Cleveland. LeBron knew people would be mad and disappointed, but he wasn't prepared for the hate he received. He made a basketball decision that gave him his best shot at a title, which had always been his focus. He had to quickly put the fallout from the Decision behind him. LeBron started with no one rooting for him, then everyone rooting for him. Now for the first time in his career, he had some people rooting against him. It was a feeling LeBron did not like, but it would all be worth it for a title.

LEBRON'S BIG THREE

LeBron, Dwyane, and Chris were now called the Big Three. Fans in Miami were giddy and expected a championship in 2010–2011. But the Big Three got off to a rocky start and the Heat started the season with 8 losses and 9 wins. If the team wanted to contend, they had to play better basketball. To play better basketball, LeBron had to lead. So he called a players only meeting. After the meeting, the Heat caught fire and rattled off 12 wins in a row! During that win streak, LeBron went to Cleveland for the first time since leaving the Cavaliers. He was booed every time he touched the ball. But LeBron was able to channel that into motivation and he scored 38 points, beating his former team. The Heat was hot for the rest of the season, racking up 58 wins and the second best record in the Eastern Conference.

G.O.A.T. LEBRON JAMES

LeBron made one thing clear to his team: the playoffs were different. Many fans had been rooting against the Heat since *The Decision*. The Heat, led by the Big Three, was expected to win it all. LeBron learned time and time again that sometimes things don't go as planned.

The first two rounds of the series were smooth sailing for the Big Three. Younger, less talented teams could not compete with three bonafide superstars. If LeBron didn't score, Wade would. If Bosh couldn't grab a rebound, LeBron was there. When they fell behind, LeBron reminded them that they were best when no one believed in them. They won both series in five games.

Being the favorite in the Eastern Conference Finals was a new feeling for LeBron as they faced the Chicago Bulls, but he adjusted. The Heat shut down the league MVP, Derrick Rose, and Chicago was powerless to overcome the Heat. In fact, in game five, Rose attempted a game-tying three pointer at the buzzer to keep the series alive. As Rose released the ball, LeBron James leapt up and got a hand on the ball. There would be no game 6. For the first time since 2007, LeBron James was heading to the NBA Finals to face the Dallas Mavericks.

LeBron opened the series as aggressive as he had been all playoffs. His teammates mimicked this. They looked to their leader for cues. LeBron spent the game

— 68 —

driving to the hoop over and over, seeing little resistance. When the Mavs attempted to contain LeBron, he passed the ball to Wade or Bosh. It looked like the Heat were on their way to an NBA championship.

In game two, the Heat was up 24 points. But somehow, Miami fell apart on defense, and the Mavericks started scoring in bunches. Wade was scoring and playing great basketball, but with eight minutes left and a 15-point lead, he started to defer to LeBron. With each possession and missed shot, LeBron saw the lead get smaller. After trailing by 24 points, the Mavericks won by two points. LeBron left the court stunned. He had to play better.

Game three found LeBron taking even less of a role on the team, so Wade and Bosh took over. The Heat came away with the road win, but something was wrong with LeBron. That became even clearer in game four. The Mavericks were playing a zone defense designed to not allow players to drive as easily. This left LeBron looking lost and hesitant on the court. He could not find his favorite shots under the basket and kept passing to teammates. He was frustrated and angry that he could not get to the foul line and could not drive into the paint. All the parts that made his game work seemed broken. As that frustration grew, he started to make mistakes, turning over the ball, badly missing shots. It all came crashing down. LeBron only scored eight points. That was a career play-off low for him. The Heat needed more out of their superstar. They lost the game and went on to lose the last two. LeBron was uninvolved and lost for most of those games as well. Once again, LeBron went to the NBA Finals and had to watch another team celebrate.

After the game, LeBron was filled with self-doubt. He spent a whole year with media and fans jeering him and rooting for him to fail. Then he did fail. Again. He started to wonder if the critics were right. For the second time, he made it to the championship to only flameout when it mattered. Was this a pattern? Did he not have what it took to be a champion? Did he really not know how to perform under pressure? He spent the offseason with all these thoughts bouncing around in his head.

LeBron eventually decided that he had two choices: dwell on his two Finals losses and let all the doubters be right, or put that all out of his mind and continue to become a better basketball player. He watched the tape from the Finals. He saw that the Mavericks shut him down by keeping him from driving to the basket. He knew exactly what he could add to his game to counteract that. He reached out to an NBA Hall of Famer, Hakeem Olajuwon. Hakeem, nicknamed the Dream, was

LEBRON'S BIG THREE

known for being an incredible **post** player. In basketball, the post is the part of the court right under the hoop. So post plays are the moves and ways to score in that area. It is an area where very big and tall players can score in bunches with the right moves. Hakeem had those moves and LeBron wanted to learn them. LeBron spent the summer with Hakeem and learned how to back down a defender and get the ball in the basket with precision footwork and crafty fakeouts. When LeBron left his last training session, Hakeem told the media that LeBron's game was finally complete. LeBron believed him.

The 2011–2012 NBA season was shortened due to a disagreement between team owners and players. They had what is called a **lockout**. The lockout was resolved, but it caused the season to start a month late and have fewer games. The Heat started the season winning games big and they never let up. The Miami Heat finished the season 46–20. LeBron once again won the regular season

LIFETIME STATS
(Per game) 12 time all star
POINTS: 21.1 x2 Finals MVP
REBOUNDS: 11.8 x2 NBA Champ
BLOCKS: 3.1 1994 MVP

MVP honors because of his improved game and incredible regular season stats. But LeBron wasn't satisfied with regular season awards anymore. He needed to win the championship.

They went into another postseason as the favorites to win the Finals. LeBron was determined not to lose. The Big Three still had last year on their mind. Every day the team would remind themselves of how bad that loss hurt. All of the Big Three took it hard. It helped them stay focused to remember the pain of the loss and to push to not experience it again. The team knew they would not have an easy road. They stumbled here and there, going down 2–1 to the Indiana Pacers in the second round before putting them away. And they were almost eliminated by the Celtics in the Eastern Conference Finals. LeBron took over the deciding game, making 12 shots in a row and scoring 45 points overall. The whole playoff run, LeBron was steady and came up big when his team needed him most. He didn't disappear and shy away from the spotlight. He stayed aggressive and averaged more than 30 points a game with 9.6 rebounds! But the real question was, would he disappear in the Finals like he did the previous year, or would he rise to the occasion?

The Heat were all set to face off against the young and exciting Oklahoma City Thunder in 2012 NBA Finals. His

LEBRON'S BIG THREE

opponents included Kevin Durant and Russell Westbrook, both of whom would go on to win MVP awards later in their careers. They were very talented and had tremendous energy. The Thunder were the second youngest team in the NBA. They played fun, fast basketball. Kevin Durant was the thoughtful, quiet leader of the team. He held the NBA scoring title for 2011–2012. Kevin Durant told the press he was going to shoot until his arms fell off, just like he did all season. He was a lethal scorer from anywhere on the court.

James Harden, Kevin Durant, and Russell Westbrook

Russell Westbrook was the team's fiery point guard. He was all attitude and swagger. Some members of the press had been critical of some of his selfish play. Westbrook shook it off, telling them he was not going to change a thing. The Thunder even had a new fan favorite player, James Harden. He was scoring over 15 points a game coming off the bench. Durant, Westbrook, and Harden were young and had something to prove. LeBron had seen this before; the Spurs and the Celtics also had superstar trios. This time, though, LeBron had his own Big Three.

G.O.A.T. LEBRON JAMES

LeBron remembered his lessons from the past two Finals. From the initial tip-off, he attacked and was aggressive. In a game with six true superstars competing, he was far and away the best player on the court. Durant tried to match him shot for shot and did well, but LeBron was playing on another level. He was determined to not let all his critics be right. He refused to disappear in the big moments but instead turned it up a notch. His teammates even noticed. Wade pointed out that in the series LeBron was driving straight to the basket. When he did that, he was like a freight train. Defenders had no chance of stopping him. The best they could do was foul him. Meanwhile, his teammates were playing great. Chris Bosh ripped down almost 10 boards a game. Dwyane Wade scored an average of 22 points per game, and took the scoring pressure off LeBron. Together as teammates, they made each other better.

There were even heroics from role players on the team. Young Mario Chalmers, nicknamed Rio by the team, came out of nowhere to win them game 4. Rio had been in the league a few years, but was not a star. Then LeBron took the young point guard under his wing. With that leadership, his confidence bloomed. Down the stretch in the fourth quarter, Rio made a driving layup past OKC's best defender and then the very next play made two clutch

LEBRON'S BIG THREE

free throws. LeBron didn't need the spotlight. He knew when to let one of his teammates shine.

The whole series, LeBron could hear Tim Duncan's words: someday this league will belong to you. Was this finally the someday he was waiting for? Was it all worth it? He had failed on the biggest stage. He had disappointed fans. He went back to the drawing board over and over to add new skills to his game. Every time he failed, he asked himself how he could be better. His best teacher was not a coach or even his mother. Instead, his best teacher was failure itself. Every time he fell down, he got back up and learned from it.

As the clock ticked down in game five of the 2012 NBA Finals, LeBron looked up at the scoreboard. He notched another triple double and the Heat dominated the game. All series he led his team in almost every category. He never let up and stayed aggressive, even when the team was down. He never got lost or doubted himself. LeBron didn't even think about the doubters. He just thought about playing his game, the one he painstakingly crafted over 9 years in the NBA. As the last second ticked away from the last game of the 2012 NBA season, it was also a countdown of the final second when LeBron James was not a champion. 3 . . . 2 . . . 1 . . . The buzzer rang and the confetti dropped and LeBron James could finally call himself a champion.

G.O.A.T. LEBRON JAMES

LeBron, Dwayne Wade, and Chris Bosh after winning their first championship with the Heat

Everything LeBron learned, every summer spent in the gym, every night lying awake replaying losses in his head, lead to that moment. His only goal since coming to the NBA was to win an NBA championship. Every decision he made was for this. He spent two Finals standing by and watching another team hoist the trophy. Now it was his turn. After all the hype and expectation, the league finally belonged to LeBron. Standing with Wade and Bosh, LeBron held the Larry O'Brien trophy high above his head for thousands of his cheering fans to see.

The Heat's Big Three would take all that momentum

and carry it into the next year. The team posted one of the most impressive regular seasons ever. At one point, they won 27 games in a row, the third-longest winning streak in NBA history! LeBron was once again brilliant, averaging 26.8 points, 8 rebounds, and 7.3 assists. He was the MVP again. It seemed like he might be the MVP forever!

The Heat went into the playoffs with 66 wins under their belt, the most in Heat franchise history. It tied the most ever by a LeBron-led team. They opened the playoffs with a tidy sweep of the Chicago Bulls and kept up their great play until the Finals. It was the Big Three's third Finals in a row. They played the San Antonio Spurs, who had a Big Three of their own in Tony Parker, Tim Duncan, and Manu Ginóbili. LeBron was familiar with them. They dealt him his first real NBA heartbreak, the sweep in the 2007 NBA Finals.

LeBron wanted payback. It took seven games. It almost didn't happen. Gregg Popovich, the Spurs coach, had devised a plan to deal with LeBron. The defense was ordered to play off LeBron and dare him to shoot jumpers. If he started to drive, they could collapse, but they were willing to let him take all the long shots he wanted. It was a gamble. Still they thought it gave them the best chance. LeBron didn't realize it at first. He said he went to watch tape of the first two games and saw what they were doing. He immediately took advantage of it, taking as many threes and long jumpers as they'd give him. It ended up burning the Spurs. LeBron scored 37 points in the pivotal game seven with five three pointers. All the work and hours in the gym practicing to fill that hole in his game paid off again. LeBron was a back to back NBA champion.

The next season (2013–2014) was another great one, but not quite as great as the one before. LeBron hit his career averages with 27 points, 7 rebounds, 6 assists for the season, and he even set a personal best when he scored 61 points against the Charlotte Bobcats. But his teammates were having trouble. They finished the season 2nd in the East with 54 wins. LeBron found himself having to carry a team again. In fact, in the playoffs, LeBron and his teammates struggled to overcome the Indiana Pacers, needing LeBron to hit a buzzer beater to win game 1. They eventually won the series but in an interview, LeBron compared it to the "Cleveland Days." Despite the struggles, the team made their fourth Finals in a row! But the celebration was short-lived. The Heat lost to the Spurs 4–1, one more lost championship to his old rivals.

After this disappointing season, LeBron had another decision to make. His contract was up and he was feeling homesick. Winning with his friends in Miami was fun, but he wanted to do something for his hometown team, too. After all, he was just a little kid from Akron at heart. Years earlier, the promise of a championship in Cleveland was made. He knew he was the only person who could deliver it to them. It would take a G.O.A.T. to bring a title to a Cleveland sports team. LeBron packed his bags. For the 2014–2015 season, he was heading back home to the Cavs.

8

RETURN OF THE KING

During the summer of 2014, LeBron wrote an essay for *Sports Illustrated* explaining why he was coming back home. He wanted to win a championship for his hometown. The King returned to a Kingdom in shambles. All the progress he had made for the Cleveland franchise was gone. The team was again losing 50+ games a season. They were floundering. Even though it had a promising young guard, Kyrie Irving, the team was still bad. LeBron wasted no time recruiting All-Star-caliber talent to come play with him. Superstar power forward Kevin Love came to Cavaliers as part of a trade. LeBron, Love, and Kyrie formed a new Big Three for Cleveland. This time LeBron knew exactly what it took to win a championship. This time he wasn't doing it for himself. He was doing it for Cleveland.

RETURN OF THE KING

LeBron and company were an offensive juggernaut. They crushed teams with exciting alley-oops and huge dunks. LeBron finally had the help he had always wanted in Cleveland, and it showed. LeBron missed a long stretch of games for the first time in his career, but the team still managed to win and make the playoffs. Their first matchup? The Boston Celtics. The last time the Cavaliers met them in the playoffs, Boston beat them badly.

Like the Cavs, the Celtics had a new roster full of young players. LeBron still showed no mercy. His team took strong leads and never let up. LeBron averaged 27 points and 9 rebounds in the series as Cleveland sept Boston.

The next two series were also relatively easy. The Cavs beat the Bulls in 6 games and swept the Hawks. Then came the Finals. LeBron had been there before. In a Cavs uniform, too. But the Cavs had never had a team this good. Kyrie Irving was averaging 21 points a game. Kevin Love was putting up nearly 20 points and 10 rebounds a game. The team seemed a lock to finally bring a championship to Cleveland.

But they were matched up against the new young superstars in the Golden State Warriors. Led by that season's sharpshooting MVP, Steph Curry, the Warriors jumped out to an early 1–0 series lead. Then LeBron came storming back in game 2, winning on the road in another

G.O.A.T. LEBRON JAMES

LeBron on the Cavs, dribbling against Steph Curry

overtime game. This was the first time in history the first two games of the Finals went to overtime. LeBron posted a triple-double with 39 points, 16 rebounds, and 11 assists. He even hit a bunch of free throws in the closing seconds of OT to seal it.

They went back to Cleveland. Cav's fans were sure this was finally their year. LeBron didn't disappoint. In game 3, the Cavaliers never trailed and LeBron scored 40 points in his first Finals in Cleveland in 8 years. But the very next game, the Cavaliers were blown out on their home court. The series was now tied 2–2. Home court advantage went back to the Warriors. The Cavs were demoralized heading back to San Francisco.

RETURN OF THE KING

LeBron scored his second triple-double of the series in game 4. He poured in 40 points, grabbed 14 rebounds, and dished out 11 assists, but it wasn't enough. Golden State won another blowout. The Cavs had to win game 6, or else the season was over. They were down for much of the game but fought back to within 4 points late, but lost 105–97. LeBron was once again defeated in the Finals. He played better than anyone could have asked him to play. He averaged 35.8 points, 13.3 rebounds, and 8.8 assists. Those stats had some wondering if LeBron should get the Finals MVP in a losing effort, something that has only happened once in NBA history. Instead Andre Iguodala of Golden State took the trophy while LeBron and his team regrouped for the next season. LeBron was determined to deliver on his promise to bring a championship to Cleveland.

The 2015–2016 season was routine for LeBron and the Cavs. Then their head coach was replaced halfway through by Tyronn Lue, even though the team was winning consistently. Lue was one of the most respected assistant coaches in the league. Many called him a "players' coach" because he got along with the players so well. He was a welcome change for LeBron and the team. The Cavs went on to win 57 games and were healthy for the playoffs. Fans were excited, but nervous . . . until the first round got underway.

G.O.A.T. LEBRON JAMES

The Cavaliers swept the first two rounds. They hardly ever trailed in a game. It was as if they had saved all their fire for the playoffs. They didn't lose a game until game 3 of the Eastern conference Finals against Toronto. 10 straight wins in the playoffs! LeBron spent much of that stretch letting young Kyrie shine. The point guard had great talent. LeBron, as always, was happy to make a teammate better. LeBron only averaged 23 points. He knew that getting the ball to Kyrie would help.

They put away the Raptors in 6 games. Then they found out who they would meet in the Finals. None other than the Golden State Warriors, again! This was LeBron's 6th straight Finals appearance—four with the Heat, and now two with the Cavs. He was ready.

The series did not start the way Cleveland wanted. The Warriors took game 1, capitalizing on a 29 to 9 run in the 3rd quarter. LeBron was in Finals mode, though. He was one assist short of a triple-double with 23 points, 12 rebounds, and 9 assists. Game 2 was worse. LeBron struggled and had 7 turnovers. Something was wrong. They lost by 33 points.

Teams that go down 0–2 in a series lose 91% of the time. It is a stat that every basketball player knows. If Cleveland didn't win game 3, they were toast. No one has ever come back from a 0–3 start.

RETURN OF THE KING

Game 3 had everything on the line. So, the Cavs opened the game with a 9–0 run and never trailed. They won the game by 30 points. LeBron had 32 points in the rout. The excitement didn't last long, though. The Cavs lost game 4 at home. It was a rough game, where LeBron and Warriors forward Draymond Green almost got in a fight. It looked like the Cavs were falling apart again. They needed to win two games on the road and one at home. Could they do it?

They went to the Oakland arena knowing what needed to be done. LeBron and Kyrie came out and played the best two-man game of their short careers together. They were unstoppable. By the end of the game, they both had 41 points. It was the first time two players on the same team had more than 40 points in the Finals. The Cavs had won on the road. It was now 3 games to 2.

They went home to Cleveland. LeBron played ferociously in game 6. At one point, late in the 3rd quarter, LeBron scored 18 points in a row. He could not be stopped. And when Steph Curry was on a breakaway trying to score a layup, LeBron chased him down and pinned the ball to the glass. LeBron had spent all of game 6 trying to frustrate Curry. He knew tough play would get under Steph's skin, just like it did to LeBron when he was new to the league. It seemed LeBron had finally done it when Curry threw his mouth guard in frustration. He

G.O.A.T. LEBRON JAMES

LeBron blocking Steph Curry

was given a technical foul and, more importantly, LeBron knew he had gotten in Steph's head. Steph Curry was blocked six times in the game and ended up fouling out.

With LeBron pushing hard at the reigning MVP, he was filling up his own box score. LeBron had liked his stats from the night before so much he did it again, scoring 41 points for the second game in a row. The Cavs won by 14, forcing a game 7 in Oakland. This was the closest any Cleveland sports franchise had been to a title in decades. There was just one game left to decide the Cavs' fate.

Playing a game 7 is the most intense feeling in basketball. It is do or die. Every single move, every shot, every practice of the season have all led to this one game.

RETURN OF THE KING

LeBron was prepared to finally deliver on his promise. He came back to Cleveland for a reason. He didn't come to lose in the NBA Finals. LeBron James came home so the city of Cleveland could witness an NBA championship. The game was close the whole way. It had 20 lead changes and 11 ties. The most important play for LeBron wasn't on offense, though. In the final 2 minutes, LeBron delivered one of the most iconic moments of his career. Andre Iguodala was on a fast break, streaking for the basket. No one was there to defend. LeBron knew it was up to him to stop Iguodala. He dug deep and sprinted after him. *Don't give up, don't give up,* was all he thought while chasing down the swift Iguodala. It was a tie game and Iggy's shot would put the Warriors up. LeBron chased him down, soaring in, seemingly out of nowhere. He took his big right hand and pinned the layup to the glass, and JR Smith grabbed the rebound. LeBron never gave up, not on the game, and not on his dream to bring a championship to Cleveland.

With the game tied, LeBron deferred to Kyrie again. He trusted the young point guard to make the right decision, and he did. Kyrie went right at Steph Curry. He dribbled, crossed over, and then stepped back. He shot a long three, letting it fly over the head of the league MVP. Swish. Kyrie drained it with 10 seconds left. Steph Curry

G.O.A.T. LEBRON JAMES

rushed back to try and answer, but his shot clanked it off the rim. The game was over. Cavs 93, Warriors 89.

LeBron and his teammates had done it. They had ended a 50+ year championship drought for the city of Cleveland. With all LeBron's firsts and records and awards, none compared to this. The one goal he set when he entered the NBA was finally checked off. He had done something that no athlete in any sport had done in over 50 years. The native son had given the people of Cleveland a championship. He wasn't just the G.O.A.T., he was a hometown hero.

9

AWARDS AND RECOGNITION

A G.O.A.T. is a once-in a lifetime player. It makes sense then that a G.O.A.T. would fill the record books and win lots of awards. LeBron definitely does both of these things. He could fill a museum with his awards and a library with the books about his play. Since he was a high school student, LeBron James has been smashing records and leaving his mark on the sport of basketball. Here are just *some* of the awards he has won.

• • •

Three Time NBA Champion

Three Time Finals MVP

Four Time NBA Most Valuable Player

14 Time NBA All Star

2004 Rookie of the Year

2008 Scoring Champion

Two Time All Star Game Most Valuable Player

38 Time Eastern Conference Player of the Month

14 Time All NBA

61 Time Eastern Conference Player of the Week

6 Time All Defensive Team

These are just the trophies and awards given out by the NBA. He won even more in the Olympics and high school.

2 Time Olympic Gold
Medalist (2008, 2012)

2012 USA
Basketball Male
Athlete of the Year

1 Time Olympic Bronze
Medalist (2004)

He collected quite a few trophies before he ever went pro. Here is his collection from before he even turned 18.

2003 National Champion

2003 Naismith Prep Player of the Year

Three Time State Champion

Two Time Gatorade Player of the Year Trophy

Two Time *USA Today* Player of the Year

Three Time Mr. Basketball

When you win as much as LeBron does, the media takes notice. Here are awards given to him by the press:

26 Times on the cover of *Sports Illustrated*

Two Time *Sports Illustrated* Sportsman of the Year

17 Time ESPY Recipient

2 Time AP Athlete of the Year

10

RECORDS AND STATS

LeBron James is the only player who has been able to play his style of basketball. The stats don't lie. He has broken records and been the first to do things people thought impossible. His career stats are so uniquely his, many fans will call getting 27 points, 7 rebounds, and 7 assists, a "LeBron." But LeBron's stats are more than just his averages. A **statistician** keeps track of a player's points, rebounds and assists, but they know so much more. They can use those numbers to show how good a player is at defense or offense. They can use numbers to tell you how many wins a player added to his team. They can show you how much better he is than the average player at his position. Statistician should be short for Stat Magician.

CAREER STATS	G	PTS	TRB	AST	FG%	FG3%	FT%	EFG%	PER	WS
L. James	1443	27.2	7.4	7.2	50.4	34.4	73.9	54.0	27.7	219.4

For his career, it is easy to see that LeBron has averaged 27.2 points, 7.4 rebounds, and 7.2 assists, which are astounding numbers. He's the first and only player to do it for his career! In fact, he seems to get better as he gets old, since in the 2016-2017 season, he was the only player ever to average at 25 points, 8 assists, 8 rebounds on 54% shooting.

As you might expect, a G.O.A.T. will have great stats in the five main categories. Here is where LeBron falls all time, as of the 2017–2018 season, and he still has a bunch more time left in the NBA.

REGULAR SEASON

POINTS: 31,425 career points (5th place)
ASSISTS: 8,208 career assists (11th place, 1st place for Forwards)

PLAYOFFS

POINTS: 6,911 career playoff points (1st all time, nearly 1,000 more than Michael Jordan, who has 5,987 in his career)

But what are those stats in the end? What is a PER, or Player Efficiency Rating, or WS, Win Share? What do those numbers mean? Why do they exist at all?

Stats like PER, WS, and VORP all sound like nicknames for Martians, but they are actually what are called advanced metrics, used to tell how much better a player makes his team. Sometimes the five basic stats (points, rebounds, assists, steals, and blocks) don't tell the whole story, so statisticians use lots and lots of math to fill in the rest.

PLAYER EFFICIENCY RATING, OR PER

The main five stats really only tell you about the good things players do. How many points someone has can be better or worse, depending on how many shots they missed to make those points. And an assist is less helpful if you also turned the ball over just as many times. The PER takes into account all the good things a player does, like score points, snatch rebounds, or get nasty blocks, and averages it out with all the bad things a player does, like miss a shot, not get back on defense, or turn the ball over. These numbers are then averaged out. If you added all the leagues' PERs together and averaged them, they would be 15. 15 is a totally normal NBA player. Not special, but not bad either. The higher the PER is than 15, the better a player is. Most All-Stars have PERs higher than 22. Most MVPs have a 26 or higher.

So how does LeBron stack up? LeBron has the second highest career PER in history. LeBron has an average PER

RECORDS AND STATS

of 27.68, just a few decimal points away from Michael Jordan at 27.91. This means throughout LeBron's career, not only does he do a lot of good things for his team, he limits his mistakes.

WIN SHARE, OR WS

Win share is what it sounds like. It is how many wins a player is directly responsible for. If a team wins 50 games in a season, the star of the team will usually be responsible for about 5 to 10 of those. This stat can of course be negative, but really excellent players will have high win shares. The math is very complicated, but is a lot like PER. Statisticians add up the good things, subtract the bad things, and then figure out how many of the season's wins a player is responsible for. This has the advantage of also telling not just who scores a lot of points, but who wins a lot of games. If you combine the Win Share of every player on a team, it will always add up to how many total wins the team had. So, if a team doesn't win very many games, the players will have a lower Win Share. LeBron James is the master of this stat. Right now he sits at 5th all time, but has a lot of games left in his career. He's only 60 WS behind Hall of Famer, Kareem Abdul Jabbar (219.36 to 273.41), and LeBron gets between 10 and 20 WS a season. For example, during the 2016–2017 season, his WS was 12.9 but he's had seasons as high as 20.3.

VALUE OVER REPLACEMENT PLAYER, OR VORP

This one is silly to say, VORP. Go ahead, say it out loud. But this is one of the most useful stats. It is not fair to compare assist numbers of a center and a point guard since their jobs are different. So this stat compares a player to an average player at the same position. This can be negative, meaning the player is worse than average, but for great players like LeBron, the VORP can be very high. LeBron James holds the highest VORP of all time, meaning that he is the most valuable player at his position compared to an average player in the same position.

Now you know some advanced stats, so when you see a PER, WS, or VORP next to a basketball player's name, you will know what they mean. You'll also know that LeBron is the King of those stats.

11

RIVALRIES

Every great athlete has rivals. They come with the territory. Everyone wants to beat the best. How could anyone be the G.O.A.T. without winning against other great players? Some rivalries only last a few games, but some last entire careers. Here are a few of LeBron's best rivalries to date. Let's see how things went for the players brave or crazy enough to try and take LeBron's crown.

LeBron and Carmelo Anthony

G.O.A.T. LEBRON JAMES

LEBRON VS CARMELO

PLAYER	PTS	REB	AST	WINS
LeBron James	25.7	7.2	7.6	18
Carmelo Anthony	22.4	6.3	3	12

LeBron James vs. Carmelo Anthony

Carmelo is LeBron's oldest rival. They played each other in high school! In their first matchup, when they were just kids, Carmelo's team won the game with LeBron scoring 36 and Anthony scoring 34. They both came into the league the same year, play the same position, and were each other's main competition for Rookie of the Year. It is hard to believe, but LeBron wasn't a unanimous pick. He actually barely beat out Carmelo, who also had a very good rookie year. After that rookie season, it was all LeBron. James has 14 All Stars, 14 All NBA teams, and a slew of other awards to Carmelo's 10 All Stars and 6 All NBA teams. LeBron also owns him in regular season head to head games 19 to 13. The only time the two met in the playoffs, LeBron's team beat Anthony's 4 games to 1. Carmelo was an early rival for Lebron but it became clear very early that LeBron was the better player.

RIVALRIES

LEBRON VS TIM

PLAYER	PTS	REB	AST	WINS
LeBron James	26.4	6.5	6.6	10
Tim Duncan	18.3	9.4	2.8	10

LeBron James vs. Tim Duncan

Some might say LeBron's rivalry isn't with future Hall of Famer Tim Duncan specifically, but with his entire team, the San Antonio Spurs. The Spurs are title contenders every year, so LeBron isn't the only player they have caused heartache. The Spurs have beaten LeBron in the Finals twice, including his first trip to the Finals in 2006–2007. Both times Tim Duncan, led the Spurs to victory. LeBron got his revenge with his second championship in Miami, but how do these two match up? Well, it is hard to say. In the regular season, LeBron fills up the box score more effectively than Tim, leading him in all categories except rebounds and blocks. But the stat that puts LeBron ahead the most is the head-to-head record. In the regular season, LeBron and Tim are tied, 10–10, but in the postseason, Duncan holds an 11–5 advantage. LeBron has better numbers, but Tim won more of their games. Plain and simple, the Spurs always had a better supporting cast and it shows in this rivalry. LeBron played the better individual game, but Tim had the better teammates. Not all rivalries go the King's way, and there is a great argument for Tim Duncan as G.O.A.T.

LEBRON VS DESHAWN

PLAYER	PTS	REB	AST	WINS
Lebron James	25.2	7.3	6.2	21
DeShawn Stevensen	8.6	2.2	1.9	6

LeBron James vs. DeShawn Stevensen

Some rivals like Duncan are evenly matched and push the player to the brink, while others are so one sided, it does not seem fair. DeShawn Stevenson was the first player to really go out of his way to pester a young LeBron. LeBron's first two appearances in the playoffs were against Stevenson, who did everything he could to get under the young prodigy's skin. Poor Stevenson didn't know that his behavior would just make LeBron play even harder. LeBron made easy work of Stevenson, who was matched up to defend LeBron, scoring big on him

RIVALRIES

in the playoffs while holding Stevenson to an average of 33% shooting. LeBron tightened his defense and exploded offensively whenever he played the Wizards. His playoff record against DeShawn is 10–6, winning both series where Stevenson was a starter and LeBron's primary defender. This rivalry defined Stevenson's career, but it is likely that LeBron barely ever thinks about it now.

LEBRON VS PAUL

PLAYER	PTS	REB	AST	WINS
LeBron James	29.3	6.7	6.5	18
Paul Pierce	20.2	5.2	3.9	21

LeBron vs. Paul Pierce

Paul Pierce versus LeBron James was the matchup to watch from 2008 to 2014. The two gladiators would battle it out in the playoffs several times during that stretch. LeBron has long rejected the idea of rivals, despite having so many, but when asked by NBA TV, he said, "I think the closest thing I have to one is Paul Pierce." At the height of their rivalry, games were not the Celtics versus the Cavaliers, but simply Paul versus LeBron.

In 2008, the Celtics-Cavaliers series went to game 7. The winner would go to the NBA Finals. The two NBA superstars butted heads the entire game. LeBron tried to will his team to a win with 45 points in that game, but Pierce shot back with 41 of his own. He sent the Celtics to the Finals and eventually won the championship.

LeBron went home knowing it was not the last he'd see of Paul Pierce. Two years later, they met again in the now famous Eastern Conference Semifinals. Pierce focused all his energy on defending LeBron and didn't even try offensively since, according to him, he was too tired from defending LeBron. He held LeBron to 34% shooting, the Cavaliers lost, and it was the loss that triggered LeBron to leave for Miami. Some might say that fans have Paul Pierce to thank for the Miami Big Three team. The very next season, Paul ran into a newly energized LeBron with a better supporting cast and the Heat beated the Celtics 4 games to 1. The very next year, Pierce was the one looking for redemption when he hit several huge shots to take the series lead in game 5. Game 6

LeBron, on the Heat, shooting against Paul Pierce

RIVALRIES

was win or go home, but LeBron scored 45 points and 15 rebounds to send them to game 7. The rest is history as the team rolled to their second Finals and first NBA Championship.

It is hard to think of another player who has stood in LeBron's way more than Paul Pierce. LeBron eventually persevered and holds a 17 to 13 edge in playoff games against Paul, but it took a while. When asked what playing Paul Pierce meant to him, LeBron said Paul put pressure on him to improve. That's what a good rival does: makes you strive to be better.

LEBRON VS DURANT

PLAYER	PTS	REB	AST	WINS
LeBron James	28.8	7.1	6.6	14
Kevin Durant	28.9	6.8	3.7	4

LeBron vs. Kevin Durant

This rivalry is just getting started. LeBron and Durant are close friends who often work out together in the off season, but that does not mean they don't play each other hard in the regular season. Since they have spent

103

their entire careers in opposite conferences, during the playoffs, they only face off in the NBA Finals. Their regular season stats are incredible though. Both players go above and beyond when facing each other. Durant came into the league a few years after LeBron and has spent much of his career trying to shake comparisons to the King. Durant has said in interviews, he hopes to someday get out of LeBron's shadow. So far, Durant has not been able to do that. LeBron has dominated him in the regular season matchup, 14 games to 6. On the other hand, they have met in the NBA Finals three times. The first time, Durant was with the Thunder and LeBron and the Heat managed them easily. In 2016, Durant was sick of not getting to the Finals and left the team that drafted him to join a team to win a championship. Sound familiar? LeBron did the same thing!

Durant's first season with the Warriors matched him in the Finals against LeBron and the Cavaliers, the 3rd matchup in a row between the powerhouse teams. Durant got his revenge when he repeated this feat the very next year. Durant holds the NBA Finals edge over LeBron with two wins to one. We have to look to the future to see what will become of this rivalry, as it is just now heating up.

RIVALRIES

LEBRON VS STEPHEN

PLAYER	PTS	REB	AST	WINS
LeBron James	31.4	10.5	8.0	13
Stephen Curry	23.4	5.1	6.5	17

LeBron vs. Stephen Curry

LeBron's rivalry with Stephen Curry is intense and ongoing. LeBron's 31.7–10.2–8.3 averages against Steph are way higher than his actual career averages. Much of this has to do with the two meeting in the Finals over and over. The NBA Finals bring out a competitive spirit in both players. They've met in the finals four times in a row! Steph has won three and LeBron has won one. Even though Steph's walked away with the trophy, LeBron clearly was the best player on the court. His averages were some of the best the game had ever seen. This included his dominating defensive performance against Steph Curry where he blocked shot after shot in the 2016 Finals. 2016 is also when LeBron won his first Finals in a Cleveland Cavaliers uniform.

Steph Curry has won more games against LeBron, but has rarely outplayed him. If you look at head to

G.O.A.T. LEBRON JAMES

head stats, LeBron has outscored Curry in 25 of their 34 games played. He had more rebounds in 29 of 34 and more assists in 24 of 34. LeBron has dominated nearly every head to head matchup between the two players. Yet, Curry has more wins because he has had the better supporting cast, including Defensive Player of the Year Draymond Green, and future Hall of Famer (and LeBron rival), Kevin Durant.

NBA fans hope this rivalry continues. The games they play against each other are electric, like the 2017–2018 All-Star Game. LeBron won, hitting the go-ahead layup in a thrilling finish. LeBron didn't get to relish that win for long since Curry defeated him in the 2017–2018 NBA Finals. Now that LeBron is with the Lakers, Curry and he share a division. This means even more regular season matchups and an almost certainty that they will see each other in the playoffs again. Only time will tell if LeBron edges out Curry in the most important stat: wins.

12

WHO ELSE?

So is LeBron the G.O.A.T.? He certainly has the resume. He isn't the only one that people think could be the G.O.A.T. though. Lots of NBA players have won championships. Many have outstanding records. Here are a few who could also be considered the greatest of all time.

BILL RUSSELL (1956–1969)

Bill Russell last played in the NBA almost 50 years ago. His imprint on the game is still felt today though. He won the NBA title eight times in a row! He was in the league for 13 years and won 11 championships in that time. Russell holds the record for the most championship titles of any player in any American sports league. He averaged more than 22 rebounds a game and was the centerpiece of one of

G.O.A.T. LEBRON JAMES

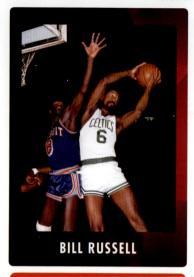

BILL RUSSELL

LIFETIME STATS
(Per game)   x12 all star
POINTS: 15.1   x5 MVP
REBOUNDS: 22.5   x11 NBA Champ
ASSISTS: 4.3   Hall of Fame

the winningest teams in history. However, the league was very different in the '50s and '60s. For one, for most of the NBA players, basketball was a part time gig and they had other jobs. The game was not on TV every night, because TV was a brand new invention! His rebounds are high, some critics say, because less talented shooters missed more shots. More missed shots mean more rebounds. In fact, if you look at the PER stat talked about in the last chapter, Bill Russell's PER was only 18.8, much lower than LeBron's. But 11 titles in 13 years is a great feat regardless of the era.

Off the court, Russell was almost more impressive. The Civil Rights Movement happened during Russell's NBA career. He was active and outspoken in an era where many athletes wanted to keep their heads down. In 1963, he marched with Martin Luther King, Jr. in the historic March on Washington demanding civil rights for African Americans. For this alone, Bill Russell certainly deserves to be in the conversation for G.O.A.T.

WHO ELSE?

MAGIC JOHNSON (1979–1991)

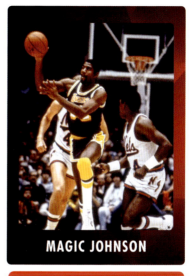

MAGIC JOHNSON

LIFETIME STATS
(Per game) x12 all star
POINTS: 19.5   x3 MVP
REBOUNDS: 7.2 x5 NBA Champ
ASSISTS: 11.2

Earvin "Magic" Johnson is a name that often comes up when talking about LeBron. Magic was a big, fast, great passer and could play every position. At point guard, he averaged for a career more than 11 assists. He made everyone around him better. He also had the best supporting cast of any player on this list. He spent much of his career playing with the NBA'S all-time leading scorer, Kareem Abdul-Jabbar.

Magic's stats were impressive, but his game was one to witness. He led the Lakers, who were a high scoring team known for their laid back plays. He didn't score as much as other people on this list. He didn't have to. Some say his defense wasn't as good as some others who would be considered G.O.A.T. This may be true and is reflected by his PER of 24.1. That puts him at 13th overall, far behind LeBron.

Magic retired in 1991 after being diagnosed with HIV. He

started the Magic Johnson Foundation to raise awareness about HIV/AIDS. Since then, the foundation has expanded to include scholarships and community empowerment centers for disadvantaged urban areas. He spent his basketball career assisting and continued to do that after retiring.

KAREEM ABDUL-JABBAR (1969-1989)

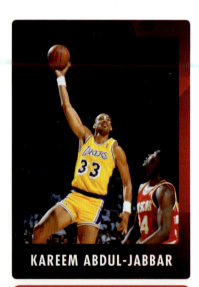

KAREEM ABDUL-JABBAR

LIFETIME STATS
(Per game) x19 all star
POINTS: 24.6 x6 MVP
REBOUNDS: 11.2 x6 NBA Champ
ASSISTS: 7.6

Where to start with Kareem? His G.O.A.T. resume is obvious. He has the most All-Star selections in history with 19. He has the most MVPs with 6. He is a six-time NBA champion. He holds the record for most career points with 38,387. He also has the record for career wins, blocked shots, and field goals made. His G.O.A.T. status for some is a no brainer and he is considered the best player of the '70s and '80s.

Kareem invented the "sky-hook" shot that almost every

WHO ELSE?

big man in the NBA learns now. He changed the game forever. He also played for 20 years, one of the longest careers in NBA history. He was incredibly consistent over those 20 years. Much like some of the others, his advanced stats are a mixed bag. His Win Shares is the most in history, mostly due to his very long career, but his PER is not even in the top 5. He's 11th actually.

• • •

So if we're going by advanced stats, who would have the best claim to G.O.A.T. other than LeBron? You've probably already guessed.

MICHAEL JORDAN
(1984–1993, 1995–1998, 2001–2003)

Air Jordan is a worldwide cultural phenomenon like no other NBA player before or since. His shoes and jerseys are still top sellers, even though he hasn't played professional basketball since 2003. He is a legend, plain and simple. It is often said that Jordan was one of the only complete basketball players ever. He had huge athleticism with a 50 inch vertical leap. He could shoot from anywhere on the floor. He was the best defender in the

G.O.A.T. LEBRON JAMES

LEBRON VS JORDAN

PLAYER	MINS	PTS	REB	AST	STL	BLK	PER
LeBron James	41,688	9,105	7,788	7,561	1,765	830	27.7
Michael Jordan	41,011	32,292	6,672	5,633	2,514	893	27.9

PLAYER	FGM	FG%	3PM	3P%	FTM	FT%	PER	TS%	USG%	WS	ORTG	DRTG
LeBron James	10,548	50.2	1,483	34.2	6,525	74	27.7	58.5	31.5	207.4	116	103
Michael Jordan	12,192	49.7	581	32.7	7,327	83.5	27.9	56.9	33.3	214	118	103

league, and still averaged 30 points a game. He had the ability to will his team to win games. There is a reason he is 6–0 in the NBA Finals. His game was so dominant that there are many NBA greats who never won a championship simply because they played during the same era as Michael. Jordan is the player that LeBron is chasing. If you compare their careers at their exact career games, you'll notice how similar they are:

According to the numbers, Jordan was a better defender than LeBron, but LeBron was a better rebounder and setup man. Otherwise, their stats are very similar. Their offensive and defensive ratings are almost identical. LeBron leads Jordan in win share, 219 to 214. It is very possible LeBron will have a much longer career

WHO ELSE?

than Jordan. Many want to give the title of G.O.A.T. to Jordan just because he was a cultural icon. They remember Jordan as being the best. But LeBron's accomplishments speak for themselves. Only time will tell if he can surpass Jordan. Some say he already has since he owns Jordan in several advanced stats, including Value Over Replacement player, and is nearly identical in things like Win Share and PER. This debate could go on for years, even after LeBron retires.

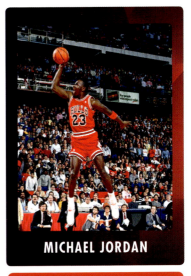

MICHAEL JORDAN

LIFETIME STATS

(Per game)	x14 all star
POINTS: 30.1	x5 MVP
REBOUNDS: 6.2	x6 NBA Champ
ASSISTS: 5.3	x10 Scoring Champ

13

WHAT THE FUTURE HOLDS

If LeBron James is not already the G.O.A.T., at the rate he is playing, he's on his way. His PER is the second best in the NBA, his Win Shares are top 5, and his Value Over Replacement Player is the best by a long shot. He is consistent with his trademark 27–7–7 average stats per season. In fact, his shooting percentage has gone up along with his assists as he's gotten older. During his 2016–2017 season, he averaged more than 8 assists, the most by a forward in history. His 2017–2018 season featured him averaging 27.5–8.6–9.1. LeBron's stats seem to keep getting better as he gets older. If LeBron continues to be healthy and play at this level, it is possible he could pass all of Jordan's records and even Kareem's records. He has several years left, barring injury. He has made 8 Finals in a row (3rd most in a row ever, tied with the

WHAT THE FUTURE HOLDS

Boston Celtics' Frank Ramsey) and doesn't seem to be slowing down.

Other than his on-court heroics, LeBron continues to be a hero for Ohio and specifically the city of Akron. In 2018, LeBron announced the opening of the IPromise school. Fully funded by LeBron and his foundation, the school is the first of its kind. It is a public school for at–risk youth. The school provides transportation, after school activities, and even a pantry the students' families can use if they are in need. LeBron and his foundation also offer job placement and GED classes for parents. Every student who graduates will have their tuition to University of Akron paid for. LeBron recognized that the only reason the little kid from Akron who slept on couches was able to become a champion was help from people in his community. He just wanted to give them the same chance he got.

At the end of the 2018 season, LeBron announced that he would take on a new goal. He won a championship in Miami. Then he came home and won one for his hometown in Ohio. His next adventure? LeBron heads to Los Angeles to bring glory back to one of the most storied franchises in all of the NBA: the Lakers. LeBron is excited about the challenge of leading a team of young players. He isn't the young superstar with limitless

G.O.A.T. LEBRON JAMES

potential anymore. Now he is a wise veteran. Many of the Lakers players grew up watching him and idolizing him. His next chapter will be that of a mentor and leader and it will be his most challenging yet. Luckily, LeBron loves a challenge.

However, many will come for the King's crown. While LeBron chases the milestones of the players who came before him, the younger players will be chasing him. Steph Curry, Kevin Durant, and James Harden are all hoping to have long careers that rival LeBron's. It is possible that 10 years from now, we will call one of them G.O.A.T. instead. Maybe the G.O.A.T. isn't even in the NBA yet. The G.O.A.T. could even be reading this book right now. Only time will tell.

LeBron Jame's reunion with the Cleavland Cavaliers ended in July of 2018 when, as a free agent, he signed a four-year deal with the Los Angeles Lakers. Can you guess how many NBA championships he will win with them?

GLOSSARY

ASSIST: A pass that leads to a teammate scoring a basket.

BACKCOURT: The half of the court behind the half court line. May also refer to a team's guards.

BLOCK: When an offensive player tips or swats a shot by an offensive player.

BOX SCORE: A collection of all statistics for all players from a single basketball.

BUZZER BEATER: A game winning shot made as time runs out.

CLUTCH: Performing well even under high pressure.

DOUBLE-DOUBLE: Getting ten or more of two stats, (e.g., 10 points, 10 rebounds)

DOUBLE TEAM: Two defenders defending one offensive player.

DRAFT: Selecting players new to the league in order based on how a team did the previous year, with the worst team picking first.

GLOSSARY

DRIBBLE: Bouncing the ball repeatedly. This is how players in basketball move the ball without passing.

DUNK: A shot made by jumping to the level of the rim and throwing it down.

EXHIBITION GAME: A game where there is nothing at stake, for example, a preseason game.

FAST BREAK: Quickly attacking the basket on offense before the defense can get in position.

FREE AGENCY: When a player is not signed to a contract with a team and can sign with any team.

G.O.A.T.: Greatest Of All Time.

JUGGERNAUT: A nearly unstoppable force.

JOURNEYMAN: An experienced and reliable player who is not a star.

NOMADIC: Living without a permanent home.

OVERTIME: The additional periods played if the score is tied at the end of the fourth quarter.

PHENOMENON: An exciting, rare person.

PRODIGY: An incredibly skilled or talented young person.

GLOSSARY

REBOUND: When a player grabs the ball after a missed shot.

REDEMPTION: Regaining a status that was lost.

RIVAL: A peer who someone competes against.

SCOUT: Someone who evaluates the skills and talent of players for college and professional teams.

SPONSORSHIP: When companies pay athletes to talk about and represent their products.

STARTER: Players who are in the game when it starts.

SWEEP: Winning a playoff series without losing a game.

STEAL: Taking the ball from an offensive player.

TRADE: An exchange of players by two teams.

TRIPLE-DOUBLE: Getting ten or more in three different stats (e.g., 10 points, 10 rebounds, 10 assists).

TURNOVER: When the offense loses the ball to the defense.

UNANIMOUS: When everyone is in agreement.

VARSITY: The highest level of high school sports teams.

VERSATILITY: The ability to play the game many different ways.

BIBLIOGRAPHY

Abrams, Jonathan. "LeBron James Accepts M.V.P. Award in His Home Town." *The New York Times.* 2 May 2010. http://www.nytimes.com/2010/05/03/sports/basketball/03lebron.html?mtrref=www.google.com.

Arnovitz, Kevin. "The First Time LeBron Dunked a Basketball." *ESPN.* March 15, 2011. Accessed May 8, 2018. http://www.espn.com/blog/truehoop/miamiheat/post/_/id/5266/the-first-time-lebron-dunked-a-basketball.

Associated Press. "LeBron James' 61 Points in Win Set Career, Heat Records." *ESPN.* March 4, 2014. Accessed May 8, 2018. http://www.espn.com/nba/recap?gameId=400489766.

Associated Press. "LeBron James Returns to Cleveland." *ESPN.* December 3, 2010. Accessed May 8, 2018. http://www.espn.com/nba/truehoop/miamiheat/news/story?id=5875623.

Associated Press. "LeBron's Playoff Debut Triple-Double Carries Cavs." *ESPN.* 23 Apr. 2006. http://www.espn.com/nba/recap?gameId=260422005.

Beck, Howard. "LeBron James Takes Game 6 Personally." *The New York Times.* June 07, 2012. Accessed May 8, 2018. https://www.nytimes.com/2012/06/08/sports/basketball/james-leads-heat-to-game-7-against-celtics.html.

Berardino, Mike. "How Hakeem Olajuwon Helped LeBron James." *South Florida Sun Sentinel.* September 22, 2012. Accessed May 7, 2018. http://articles.sun-sentinel.com/2012-09-22/sports/sfl-hakeem-helps-

BIBLIOGRAPHY

lebron-james-in-title-run-0922_1_lebron-james-heat-s-nba-finals-hakeem-olajuwon.

Boren, Cindy. "Paul Pierce Probably Won't like Being a Footnote in LeBron James' History." *The Washington Post*. May 18, 2015. Accessed May 7, 2018. https://www.washingtonpost.com/news/dc-sports-bog/wp/2015/05/17/paul-pierce-probably-wont-like-being-a-footnote-in-lebron-james-history/?noredirect.

Bowers, Brenden. "LeBron James: What He Learned About Leadership From Ricky Davis." *ThePostGame*. 4 Jan. 2018. http://www.thepostgame.com/lebron-james-ricky-davis-cavaliers-rookie-bowers.

Christopher, Matt. *On the Court with LeBron James*. New York: Little, Brown, 2016.

Cote, Greg. "Haters of Miami Heat's LeBron James Can Be Quieted for Good with Two More Wins." *Miami Herald*. June 19, 2013. Accessed May 7, 2018. http://www.miamiherald.com/sports/nba/article1940681.html.

Flannery, Jim. "NBA: The Case for Wilt Chamberlain as the Best Ever." *Bleacher Report*. April 12, 2017. Accessed May 8, 2018. http://bleacherreport.com/articles/1217186-nba-the-case-for-wilt-chamberlain-as-the-best-ever.

Freedman, Lew. *LeBron James: A Biography*. Westport, CT: Greenwood Press, 2008.

Friel, John. "2011 NBA Finals: Game-by-Game Report Card for LeBron James' Postseason." *Bleacher Report*. 3 Oct. 2017. http://bleacherreport.com/articles/734815-2011-nba-finals-game-by-game-report-card-for-lebron-james-post-season.

Gaffney, Tom. "Name Is James, LeBron James." *Akron Beacon Journal*, March 26, 2000, p 55.

Green, Mark Anthony. "Lebron James's Billion-Dollar Nike Deal Is This Guy's Doing." *GQ*. May 17, 2016. Accessed May 7, 2018. https://www.gq.com/story/lebron-james-nike-deal-bilion-maverick-carter.

BIBLIOGRAPHY

Haynes, Chris. "LeBron James on What Paul Pierce Meant to His Career: 'I Knew I Had to Become Much Better'." Cleveland.com. May 17, 2015. Accessed May 8, 2018. http://www.cleveland.com/cavs/index.ssf/2015/05/lebron_james_paul_pierce_1.html.

"Heat at Bulls." NBA.com. March 27, 2013. Accessed May 8, 2018. http://www.nba.com/games/20130327/MIACHI/gameinfo.html.

Helfand, Zach. "LeBron James Never Forgot Where He Came from and They Never Forgot Him." *Los Angeles Times.* October 27, 2014. Accessed May 7, 2018. http://www.latimes.com/sports/nba/la-sp-lebron-james-akron-20141028-story.html.

Isadore, Chris. "SportBiz: Carmelo Anthony—Still a Bargain for Advertisers." *CNNMoney.* February 5, 2004. Accessed May 7, 2018. http://money.cnn.com/2004/02/05/commentary/column_sportsbiz/sportsbiz/.

James, LeBron, and Buzz Bissinger. *Shooting Stars.* New York: Penguin Press, 2009.

"James, Nash Share Sporting News MVP Award." *ESPN.* May 12, 2006. Accessed May 07, 2018. http://www.espn.com/nba/news/story?id=2443137.

Kaufman, Michelle. "Prepped for Greatness." *Democrat and Chronicle* (Rochester, NY), December 12, 2002, p. 1D.

King, Jay. "LeBron James Considers Boston Celtics Star Paul Pierce, Not Kobe Bryant, His Greatest Rival." Masslive.com. June 5, 2013. Accessed May 8, 2018. http://www.masslive.com/celtics/index.ssf/2013/06/lebron_james_paul_pierce_bosto.html.

"LeBron James Interview." *Inside Hoops.* January 4, 2004. Accessed May 7, 2018. http://www.insidehoops.com/lebron-james-interview-010403.shtml.

"LeBron's Playoff Debut Triple-double Carries Cavs." *ESPN.* April 23, 2006. Accessed May 07, 2018. http://www.espn.com/nba/recap?gameId=260422005.

BIBLIOGRAPHY

Lee, Joon. "'He Was a Man Amongst Boys': Catching Up with LeBron James' High School QBs." *Bleacher Report*. April 12, 2017. Accessed May 8, 2018. http://bleacherreport.com/articles/2692760-he-was-a-man-amongst-boys-catching-up-with-lebron-james-high-school-qbs.

Littlefield, Bill. "Bill Russell: Champion of Basketball And Civil Rights." *WBUR News*. 21 Nov. 2013. http://www.wbur.org/news/2013/11/01/russell-basketball-civil-rights.

Maeland, Alex. "Nike Presents First Dunk: A Story about LeBron James." HYPEBEAST. August 14, 2016. Accessed May 8, 2018. https://hypebeast.com/2011/10/nike-presents-first-dunk-a-story-about-lebron-james.

Mahoney, Brian. "James, Wade Help Heat Top Thunder, Go Up 2–1 in Finals." *Star Telegram*. June 16, 2012. Accessed May 7, 2018. http://www.star-telegram.com/sports/article3831756.html.

Morgan, David Lee. *LeBron James: The Rise of a Star*. Cleveland: Gray & Company, Publishers, 2003.

NBA.com Staff. "Top Moments: LeBron James Dominates Pistons En Route to Finals." *NBA.com*. 24 Aug. 2017. http://www.nba.com/history/top-moments/2007-lebron-pistons-playoffs.

Nelsen, Chris. "LeBron James Reflects on His Palace Memories vs. Detroit Pistons." *Detroit Free Press*. 10 Mar. 2017. http://www.freep.com/story/sports/nba/pistons/2017/03/09/lebron-james-game-5-2007-east-finals/98966090/.

Neumann, Thomas. "Twelve Things You Need to Know on the 12th Anniversary of LeBron James' NBA Debut." *ESPN*. October 29, 2015. Accessed May 07, 2018. http://www.espn.com/nba/story/_/id/14002264/on-date-2003-lebron-james-made-nba-debut-cleveland-cavaliers.

Norwich, Grace, and Ute Simon. *I Am Lebron James*. New York, NY: Scholastic, 2014.

BIBLIOGRAPHY

"Oklahoma City Guard Russell Westbrook Says He Won't Change His Style." *The Seattle Times.* June 16, 2012. Accessed May 7, 2018. https://www.seattletimes.com/sports/nba/oklahoma-city-guard-russell-westbrook-says-he-wont-change-his-style-nba-playoffs/.

Pelton, Kevin. "Best Playoff Runs: Players 1–5." *ESPN.* June 10, 2013. Accessed May 08, 2018. http://www.espn.com/nba/playoffs/2013/story/_/id/9357345/greatest-individual-postseasons-1-5.

Plain Dealer Staff. "When LeBron Really Needed It, a Family Stepped in and Made a Lasting Difference: The Making of an MVP." Cleveland.com. December 6, 2009. Accessed May 8, 2018. http://www.cleveland.com/cavs/index.ssf/2009/12/when_lebron_really_needed_it_a.html.

Pluto, Terry, and Brian Windhorst. *The Franchise: Lebron James and the Remaking of the Cleveland Cavaliers.* Cleveland: Gray & Company, Publishers, 2015.

Pluto, Terry, and Brian Windhorst. *Lebron James: The Making of an MVP.* Cleveland, OH: Gray & Company, Publishers, 2009.

Reed, Tom. "Pro Scouts Drool over McDonald's." *Akron Beacon Journal*, March 25, 2003, p C1.

Saslow, Eli. "Lost Stories of LeBron, Part 1." *ESPN.* October 17, 2013. Accessed May 8, 2018. http://www.espn.com/nba/story/_/id/9825052/how-lebron-james-life-changed-fourth-grade-espn-magazine.

Shaw, David T. "Lower Merion to Begin Work on Turnaround Season." *Philadelphia Inquirer*, December 9, 1993, p. MDB7.

Sheridan, Chris. "Debut Ball: LeBron's 1st Playoff Game One to Remember." *ESPN.* 27 Apr. 2006. http://www.espn.com/nba/playoffs2006/columns/story?columnist=sheridan_chris&id=2418119.

Taylor, Ihsan. "Book Review|'Shooting Stars,' by LeBron James and Buzz Bissinger." *The New York Times.* October 1, 2009. Accessed May 8, 2018. https://www.nytimes.com/2009/10/04/books/review/Taylor-t.=collection%2Ftimestopic%2FJames%2C%2BLeBron&action=click&

BIBLIOGRAPHY

contentCollection=timestopics&region=stream&module=stream_
unit&version=search&contentPlacement=8&pgtype=collection.

Wahl, Grant. "Ahead of His Class Ohio High School Junior LeBron James is so Good That He's Already Being Mentioned as the Heir to Air Jordan." SI.com. February 18, 2002. Accessed May 8, 2018. https://www.si.com/vault/2002/02/18/318739/ahead-of-his-class-ohio-high-school-junior-lebron-james-is-so-good-that-hes-already-being-mentioned-as-the-heir-to-air-jordan.

Windhorst, Brian. "A Season without Acquittal for LeBron." *ESPN.* 13 June 2011. http://www.espn.com/blog/truehoop/miamiheat/post/_/id/8869/another-season-without-acquittal-for-lebron.

Windhorst, Brian. "The Chosen Ones." *ESPN.* June 23, 2013. Accessed May 8, 2018. http://www.espn.com/nba/draft2013/story/_/page/2003-draft-history-1/an-oral-history-2003-lottery-draft.

Winfield, Kristian. "LeBron James' Cavaliers Teammates from 2003 Had Mixed Reviews about Drafting Him." SBNation.com. May 27, 2017. Accessed May 7, 2018. https://www.sbnation.com/2017/5/27/15704514/lebron-james-rookie-teammates-carlos-boozer-cavaliers-darius-miles-smush-parker-ricky-davis.

Zillgitt, Jeff. "LeBron James Fulfills Promise to Bring a Title to Cleveland." *USA Today.* June 20, 2016. Accessed May 7, 2018. https://www.usatoday.com/story/sports/nba/playoffs/2016/06/19/cavaliers-win-nba-championship/86123514/.

INDEX

Abdul-Jabbar, Kareem, 110, 111
Anthony, Carmelo
 at Oak Hill Academy, 21
 vs. LeBron James as G.O.A.T., 97, 98
Assists, definition of, 14, 15, 117
Backcourt, definition of, 117
Basketball statistics, 14, 15
Bench, definition of, 15
Billups, Chauncy, 52, 53
Block, definition of, 117
BLK, definition of, 15
Boozer, Carlos, 31
Bosh, Chris, 64, 65, 76
Box score, definition of, 117
Bryant, Kobe,as rookie, 39
Buzzer beat, definition of, 117
Carter, Maverick, 18, 19
Chalmers, Mario, 74
Clutch, definition of, 117
Curry, Steph
 as rookie, 39
 as member of Golden State
  Warriors, 81, 82, 85, 86, 87
 vs. LeBron James as G.O.A.T.,
  105–106
Dambrot, Keith, 17
Davis, Ricky, 34, 35
Double-double, definition of, 117
Double team, definition of, 117
Draft, definition of 119
DREB, definition of, 15
Dribble, definition of, 118

Duncan, Tim
 advice to LeBron James, 55, 75
 and Big Three, 77
 vs. LeBron James as G.O.A.T., 99,
  100
Dunk, definition of, 118
Durant, Kevin
 as rookie, 38
 vs Miami Heat, 73, 74
 vs LeBron James as G.O.A.T., 102,
  103
Eastern Conference, 36
Exhibition game, definition of, 27,
 118
Fab Four, 10
Fast break, definition of, 118
FGA, definition of, 15
FGM, definition of, 15
Free agency, definition of, 44,
 118
FTA, definition of, 15
FTM, definition of, 15
G.O.A.T., definition of, 5, 6,
 118
Garnett, Kevin, 61
Ginobili, Manu, 77
Green, Draymond
Harden, James, 73
Howard, Dwight, 57
Hughes, Larry, 43, 44
Iguodala, Andre, 83
IPromise school, 115
Irving, Kyrie, 80, 81

126

INDEX

James, LeBron
  awards and recognition, 89–91
  battle with other rookies, 38–39
  childhood, 7–11
  early years with Cleveland
    Cavaliers, 29–37
  endorsements, 30
  future of, 114–116
  high school achievements, 13–28
  as most valuable player, 55–62
  moving to Miami, 63–79
  postseason achievements, 43–54
  records and stats, 92–96
  returning to Cleveland, 80–88
  rivalries, 97–106
Johnson, Magic, 108, 109
Jordan, Michael
  as G.O.A.T., 6
  Nike deal, 29, 30
  vs. LeBron James as G.O.A.T.,
    111–113
Journeyman, definition of, 118
Juggernaut, definition of, 118
Lockout, 71
Love, Kevin, 80
Lue, Tyronn, 83
Miami Heat, 67–79
Miles, Darius, 31
MIN, definition of, 15
Most Valuable Player award, 59
NBA
  All-Star Game, 41
  conferences, 36
Nomadic, definition of, 118
Oak Hill Academy, 21
Oklahoma City Thunder, 72, 73
Olajuwon, Hakeem, 70, 71
OREB, definition of, 15
Overtime, definition of, 118
Parker, Tony, 77
Personal fouls, definition of, 15
Phenomenon, definition of, 118

Pierce, Paul
  against Cleveland Cavaliers, 61
  vs LeBron James at G.O.A.T., 101,
    102, 103
Player Efficiency Rating, 93, 94, 95
Popovich, Gregg, 53, 54
Prep-to-pro player, 31
Prodigy, definition of, 118
PTS, definition of, 15
Rebounds, definition of, 14, 119
Redemption, definition of, 119
Rivalry, definition of, 22, 121
Russell, Bill, 107, 108
Scout, definition of, 119
Sponsorship, definition of, 119
St. Vincent-St. Mary's, 13, 16, 17, 18,
    19, 26, 27
Starter, definition of, 119
Steal, definition of, 15, 119
Stevensen, DeShawn, 100, 101
Stoudemire, Amar'e, 37, 39
Sweep, definition of, 119
3PT, definition of, 15
TO, definition of, 15
Trades, definition of, 44, 119
Triple-double, definition of, 40, 119
Turnover, definition of, 119
Unanimous, definition of, 119
Value Over Replacement Player, 96
Varsity, definition of, 119
Versatility, definition of, 119
Wade, Dwyane
  in Olympics with LeBron James,
    63, 64, 65
  on Miami Heat with LeBron
    James, 66, 67, 74
Walker, Frankie, 9, 10
Western Conference, 36
Westbrook, Russell, 73
Williams, Mo, 56
Win Share, 93, 94, 95, 96

IMAGE CREDITS

Alamy Stock Photo: Adam Stoltman 109, ZUMA Press Inc 39

AP Photo: © Tony Dejak 8, © Danny Moloshok 19

Getty images: Issac Baldizon/NBAE 4, 102, Andrew D. Bernstein/NBAE 113, Lisa Blumenfeld 30, Timothy A. Clary/AFP 38, Ned Dishman/NBAE 47, Garrett Ellwood/NBAE 86, 97, C.W. Griffin/Miami Herald/MCT 76, Michael Hickey 1, 71, 82, Glenn James/NBAE 73, George Long/Sports Illustrated 110, John W. McDonough 12, Filippo Monteforte/AFP 65, Adam Pantozzi/©NBAE cover, Dick Raphael/NBAE 108, Bob Rosato /Sports Illustrated 57

Courtesy Wikimedia Commons: Steve Jurvetson 66